The Campaign of Jena 1806

The Campaign of Jena 1806
Napoleon's Decisive Defeat
of the Prussian Army

J. H. Anderson

LEONAUR

The Campaign of Jena 1806
Napoleon's Decisive Defeat
of the Prussian Army
by J. H. Anderson

First published under the title
The Campaign of Jena 1806

Leonaur is an imprint of Oakpast Ltd

ISBN: 978-0-85706-443-1 (hardcover)
ISBN: 978-0-85706-444-8 (softcover)

http://www.leonaur.com

Publisher's Notes

Contents

Preface

This work deals with the Napoleonic Campaign of 1806 from August 9 to November 8 with special reference to the period from October 10 to 14. The F. S. Regulations should be considered in reference to the events of the campaign.

Authorities are: Lettow-Vorbeck's *Krieg, 1806 and 1807*; Goltz, *Jena to Eylau* with excellent maps; the work of General Bonnal, *La Manoeuvre d'Iena*; Putzger's *Historical Atlas*; Schirmer's *War Atlas*, 1792-1912; Houssaye's *Jena*; Colonel Maude's *Jena* with good maps and to it I am much indebted; Mr. Petre's *Conquest of Prussia* which I have constantly consulted and which the student desiring details should read; Horsetzky's *Campaigns since 1792*; Anderson's *Précis of Great Campaigns*; Donaldson's useful *Military History*; Alison's *History of Europe and Atlas*, and Hamley's *Operations of War*.

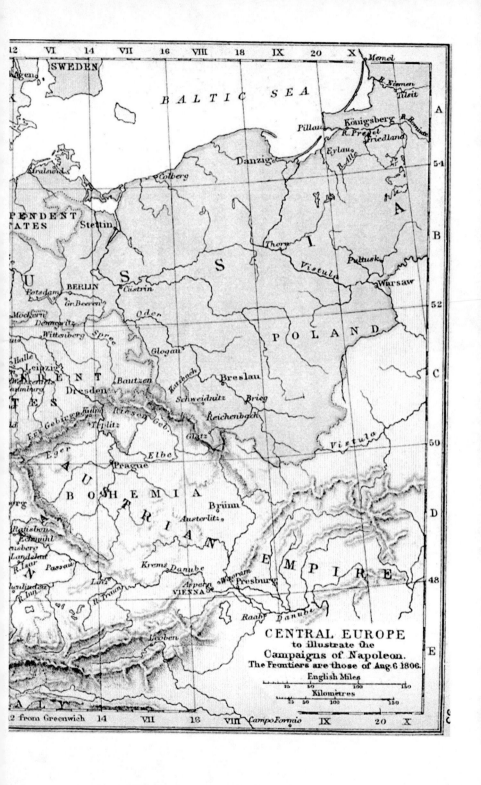

CENTRAL EUROPE
to illustrate the
Campaigns of Napoleon.
The Frontiers are those of Aug. 6 1806.

English Miles

Kilomètres

Table of Dates

1806.

August 6   Francis renounces title of German Emperor.

August 9   Berlin resolves on war.

September 19 Napoleon issues orders to his troops in South Germany.

September 25 Napoleon quits Paris. Prussian Second Plan.

October 3   French on the upper Main.

October 5   Napoleon's orders to cross the frontier.

October 7   Prussian ultimatum reaches Napoleon.

October 8   Prussian Third Plan. Skirmish at Saalburg.

October 9   Combat at Schleiz.

October 10 Napoleon's letter to Soult.
            Combat at Saalfeld.
            9 a.m. Prussian main body arrives.
            10 a.m. Suchet approaches Garnsdorf.
            11 a.m. Prince Louis rearranges his men and has Hohenlohe's message.
            1 p.m. French carry Crösten.
            Prussian Fifth Plan.

October 12 Skirmish at Göschwitz.
            Allies at Weimar—Jena.

October 13 Davout takes Naumburg.
            Napoleon's letter to Murat.
            Lannes at Jena.

11

Prussian Sixth Plan.
Napoleon on the hill.

October 14 BATTLE OF JENA.

Clock of Battle.

6 a.m.	Lannes advances.
7.45 a.m.	Gazan carries Lützeroda.
9 a.m.	Tauentzien retires.
9.15 a.m.	Ney's advanced guard arrives.
10 a.m.	St. Hilaire checks Holtzendorf. Rüchel starts.
11.30 a.m.	Holtzendorf at Stobra.
11 a.m. to 1 p.m.	Severe fighting round Vierzehnheiligen.
12.30 p.m.	Cavalry charges near Isserstedt.
1.15 p.m.	St. Hilaire arrives.
1.30 p.m.	French cavalry attack and pursue.
2 p.m.	Holtzendorf at Apolda Rüchel reaches Kapellendorf.
3 p-m.	Saxons flee on Kapellendorf. Holtzendorf crosses Ilm R.
4 p.m.	Last stand of allies near Weimar.

October 14 THE BATTLE OF AUERSTEDT.

Clock of Battle.

8 a.m.	Blücher charges.
9 a.m.	Schmettau and Friant arrive.
11 a.m.	Morand arrives. Prince William's charge.
12 noon	French offensive.

October 14 Bernadotte at Dornburg and Apolda.

October 15 The King at Sömmerda, Erfurt surrenders.

October 17 Battle of Halle.

October 20 Hohenlohe at Magdeburg.

October 21 Hohenlohe leaves Magdeburg.

October 24 Blücher crosses Elbe at Sandau.

October 25-27 Entry into Berlin.

October 26 Weimar crosses Elbe at Sandau.
Action of Zehdenick.

October 28 Surrender at Prenzlau,
Soult crosses Elbe at Tangermunde.

October 29 Stettin surrenders.

November 1 Cüstrin surrenders.
Blücher on Schwerin.

November 5 Blücher at Lübeck.

November 6 Fall of Lübeck.

November 7 Blücher surrenders.

November 8 Magdeburg surrenders.

Note

THE ERRORS OF NAPOLEON:

(1) On October 10 he thought Hohenlohe was moving against him in the Franken Wald;

(2) On October 10 he thought Hohenlohe was concentrating at Gera;

(3) On October 11 he thought that the allies were concentrating at Erfurt and that the battle would be on the 16th, hence the dangerous position of Lannes and Augereau, left of the Saale on October 12 and 13 and hence the distance of Davout from the main army (it turned out luckily); (

4) just as Hohenlohe was wrong in thinking on October 13 that Lannes and Augereau, left of the Saale, would alone attack him, so was Napoleon wrong on October 13 when he thought he had all the allies before him, for he was ignorant of Brunswick's march till the morning of October 15;

(5) he supposed the garrison of Magdeburg smaller and the retreating force of Hohenlohe larger than was the case.

CHAPTER 1

Causes of the War

From 1795 to 1806 Prussia pursued a successful policy of selfish neutrality, but in the Ulm Campaign of 1805 the French Marshal Bernadotte had violated the Prussian territory of Ansbach and even the vacillating King of Prussia, indignant at the insult, had concluded an arrangement with the Tsar and the Austrian ruler before the battle of Austerlitz, December 2, 1805. This battle however altered the tone of the Prussian King and he accepted with Napoleon the Treaty of Schönbrünn. This treaty gave Hanover, the electorate of George III, to Prussia whilst the latter resigned to France the Prussian district of Kleve east of the Rhine (this district plus the Prussian bishopric of Münster, the Mark and the Duchy of Berg—the last granted to France by Bavaria in lieu of the Prussian district of Baireuth—was formed during 1806 into the Grand Duchy of Berg for Marshal Murat), her province of Neufchâtel in Switzerland to Marshal Berthier, the celebrated Chief of Staff, and Ansbach to the King of Bavaria. The main reason for Napoleon's offer of Hanover to Prussia was that he knew acceptance would mean a Prussian war with the great maritime power.

The aristocratic and military party under the heroic and beautiful Queen Louise and prince Louis Ferdinand, the Alcibiades of Prussia, did their best to overturn the treaty, but the French Monarch insisted, the treaty was executed and the King of Prussia, an object of contempt to Europe and to none more than to Napoleon, found himself at war with Great Britain. Later on in the year the French Emperor set up under his own protection the vassal Confederation of the Rhine (Bavaria, Württemberg, Baden, Hesse-Darmstadt, Berg, etc.), a step which caused Francis II, Holy Roman Emperor of the German nation, to renounce that august title and to assume that of Francis I, Emperor of Austria, August 6, 1806.

The Confederation was also a bitter pill for Prussia and the last straw was added when she discovered that Napoleon had in negotiations with Great Britain offered to return Hanover to George III and heard a rumour that in negotiations with the Tsar he had offered to hand over Prussian Poland to that Sovereign. Besides there was the judicial murder of Palm for publishing a German patriotic book. Therefore on August 9 Berlin resolved on war and in consequence readily joined Great Britain in forming the Fourth Coalition of Great Britain, Prussia, Russia, Sweden and Saxony against France, Holland, the Confederation of the Rhine and the Kingdom of Italy.

Prussia wanted time for preparation and she got six weeks, for Napoleon, desirous of peace, perfectly aware how unready Prussia and Russia were, and scornful of the Prussian King's willpower ("He will arm and disarm") was not decided on war till September 18, and not till the 19th did he issue concentration orders for his corps in South Germany where all his Austerlitz troops, fed by forced contributions from his German vassals, had remained save only the Imperial Guard. On September 25 he left Paris to join his army, south of the R. Main, at Bamberg where on October 7 he received the Prussian ultimatum, demanding that all French troops retire beyond the Rhine. The only reply vouchsafed was the advance of the French troops.

CHAPTER 2

Theatre of Operations

To understand this campaign one must realise the following territorial frontiers: so far as concerns us Napoleon's dominions included France up to the Rhine, his brother Louis' Kingdom of Holland, and his brother-in-law Murat's Grand Duchy of Berg which ran from Wesel up the east bank of the Rhine opposite Koln; he also controlled the Confederation of the Rhine and was himself King of Italy, *i.e.* the north-eastern region of Italy.

Sweden included Swedish Pomerania round Stfalsund and very peculiar was the position of the following states:—Weimar neutral but its reigning duke a Prussian officer; Lübeck a neutral Free City but the scene of operations; the scattered Duchy of Brunswick neutral but its duke a Prussian officer; Hesse-Kassel neutral but its Elector secretly hostile to France; Mecklenburg neutral, but the scene of operations, and its Duke's daughter the Queen of Prussia. The real difficulty however is Prussia because that power meant something quite different from what it means to us. Then it included the originally Polish provinces of Old or East Prussia, West Prussia, South Prussia, New East Prussia (including Warsaw), besides Silesia, Pomerania, Brandenburg and numerous scattered bits to the west, namely, Baireuth, East Friesland, Münster, the Mark, Paderborn, Hanover, Hildesheim, Erfurt and Eichsfeld. It is well to realise that the whole Prussian population numbered only 10,000,000 as against 36,000,000 in Napoleon's dominions.

The theatre stretched from the Rhine and Main Rivers across

the Elbe to the Oder, including the Hartz Mountains, the Thuringian Wald, and the Frankenwald through which the roads are few. Particularly note the R. Saale (tributary of the Elbe, not of the Main) between which stream and Bamberg and Baireuth lies a hilly wooded country, but on the right bank of the upper Saale are many roads across a rolling *plateau* intersected by valleys, *e.g.* Pösneck to Saalfeld; the river itself flows in a deep valley, and near Leipzig stretches a plain, part of the great plain upon which the combatants entered as they approached the Elbe. This great plain covers all North Germany and in it, especially north of Berlin and in Mecklenburg, we find numerous rivers, canals and lakes. In the last phase of the campaign the operations covered Mecklenburg, Brandenburg and Pomerania, a marshy and sandy region.

CHAPTER 3

The Forces

The Prussian infantry was good but out of date and slow in movements, the French intelligent and rapid, *e.g.* for six consecutive days in the second week of October the Imperial Guard averaged eighteen miles a day. Colonel Maude, (*The Jena Campaign: 1806* by F. N. Maude, also published by Leonaur),remarks that the principal cause of French mobility was the Emperor's habit of going to bed at 8 p.m. and rising at midnight, then receiving reports and issuing orders, whereas in most armies orders were issued in the afternoon. In battle the Prussian infantry adopted close formations and deployed slowly into line before opening fire—these linear tactics failed against the mobile system of the French, who employed clouds of skirmishers backed by "small handy columns" (Maude). The skirmishers aided by artillery shook the enemy's line which was then crushed by the columns. For attack Napoleon preferred the column, for defence the line. The Prussian musket too was very inferior, says Mr. Petre, but Col. Maude, doubts this.

In artillery the Prussians knew nothing about massing of guns, a practice which Napoleon was gradually adopting, and yet in 1806 the Prussians had the greater number of gnus per 1000 infantry. A Prussian battery included either eight or twelve guns.

In cavalry (which Col. Maude states fell below the Great Frederick's standard—the result of economy—) the Prussians were tactically superior, but they foolishly thought they could successfully charge unbroken infantry, witness their defeat at Auerstedt. Strategically both cavalries were defective, *e.g.* Murat often brought incorrect information, and spies are no real substitute for cavalry reconnaissance. One great error damaged the Prussian cavalry—it was not organised independently under one leader.

In financial resources and in organisation Napoleon excelled the enemy: armies had increased since the time of the Great Frederick and in these larger armies it was a great advantage to have the French system of *corps d'armée* "each of two to five divisions and each containing from 20,000 to 30,000 men with guns, a reserve and some light cavalry; each army corps was commanded by a Marshal and the size of the army corps varied with the abilities of the Marshal. The heavy cavalry and the dragoons were separately organised under one general. The organisation of the Imperial Guard was the same except that it was considered as the reserve of the whole army and as especially under the Imperial control. Napoleon also employed highly trained light infantry to act as skirmishers.

The *esprit de corps* of the army was remarkable; and Napoleon, whilst giving general instructions to his marshals, always left them a considerable discretion which however did not mean that he did not watch every movement with unceasing vigilance, as we see in his voluminous correspondence. In one respect only the changes of Napoleon at this period were of doubtful utility, and that was in virtually suppressing the *état major* or general staff, by enacting that the rank of colonel in it should be abolished; an ordinance which, by closing the avenue of promotion, at once banished all young men of ability from that department, and degraded what had formerly been the chief school of military talent into a higher species of public couriers" (Anderson, *Napoleonic Campaign of 1805*). Note that alone of the Powers Napoleon had a semaphore telegraph from the capital to his headquarters.

Thus all Napoleon had to do was to issue instructions to his corps commanders. With the Prussians on the other hand the

Army was far more of an integer; there was no corps organisation and only a defective divisional organisation and hence increase of detail work for the commander-in-chief. The Prussian Army was not an aggregate of corps or divisions; it was an aggregate of regiments. It was no doubt perfectly drilled. Napoleon again exercised absolute control and consulted no one, whereas the Prussian commander-in-chief was worried by the King, by Rüchel and by Hohenlohe; councils of war were frequent, and though the Duke of Brunswick was a man of great capacity and immense knowledge he was dissipated and deficient in resolution.

In the matter of Staff arrangements too Napoleon had the advantage, though his own conspicuous ability reduced Berthier and the others to mere automata: the Prussian Staff system was chaos under such theorists as Phull and Massenbach, the evil genius of Prussia, and possessed no means of rapidly issuing orders, note the difference between the two commanders-in-chief on October 13.

As to the commanding generals the French were able and not advanced in years, whereas the Prussian were mostly past their work, e.g., Napoleon was thirty-seven, Brunswick seventy-one. The Prussian officers were boastful, Hohenlohe declaring "I shall beat Napoleon" and the generals stating that Bonaparte was not fit to be a Prussian corporal.

Numbers—Prussia foolishly left troops in Silesia and in Polish Prussia and out of 250,000 (217,000 according to Clausewitz) brought up only 130,000, whilst Saxony out of 50,000 brought up only 20,000; total 150,000 including 35,000 horse, with 550 guns. On the other side Napoleon had on the Upper Main 180,000 including 32,000 horse, with 300 guns; south of these 26,000 Confederation troops and some Bavarians on the R. Inn and in the Tyrol.

In the West near Mainz the 8th Army Corps under Mortier counted 24,000 (really only three French infantry regiments—Petre), and in the North in Holland were 20,000 under King Louis Bonaparte. The total of the Imperial forces ran up to

600,000 for, as Rüstow says, "France was up to 1809 the only state whose military force was the national strength regularly organised"; the Prussian Army was purely professional.

CHAPTER 4

The General Idea on Both Sides

Napoleon having as his base of operations the *reentrant* formed by the Middle and Lower Rhine and Main with their bridges had the following choices:—

(1) Move by the great high road through Mainz, Fulda, Erfurt, Leipzig to Berlin; strategic objections were that the Elbe must be crossed and the Prussians would be driven on to their Russian allies and back on their communications;

(2) Move *via* Wesel, Osnabrück, Hanover, Brunswick, Magdeburg to Berlin; objections were numerous the Weser and Elbe must be crossed, Prussians would retire on their allies and their communications, it would involve a long flank march by the Austerlitz troops, all except the Guard quartered since 1805 in South Germany, moreover Austria must be watched as long as possible for fear she might join this Fourth Coalition;

(3) From the upper Main (Bamberg and Baireuth) he could avoid the difficult Thuringian Forest by using the three roads *via* Hof , Kronach, and Coburg that run through the less difficult Franken Wald and thus would reach the upper Saale and once over it the only obstacle before reaching Berlin was the Elbe River; the strategic advantages were enormous he would either avoid the great rivers or meet them where they were not formidable (Donaldson), he would threaten the Saxon communications with Dresden and the Prussian with Magdeburg, Torgau, and Berlin, he might seize Dresden and thus control the passage of the Elbe.

In any case he would not drive the Prussians on to the Russians. The only real objections were that the Prussians might pass through the Thuringian Forest and cut his communications, if, that is to say, he was based on Mainz, and that he would pass between the enemy and the neutral frontier of Bohemia (Donaldson). This route he chose to effect his General Idea which was to crush the Prussians, occupy Dresden and Berlin, sever the Prussians from their lukewarm allies, the Saxons and both from the Russians. It is interesting to note, as Donaldson in his *Military History and Modern Warfare* remarks, that Jomini, Ney's Chief of Staff, accurately forecast the Emperor's scheme; Jomini probably judged from 1805 when Napoleon aimed to crush Mack before the Russians could arrive, just as he aimed now to crush the Prussians before the *Tsar's* battalions could appear and this Bamberg route promised an early decision.

On September 5 he began to prepare for a concentration on Bamberg and Baireuth and to obtain information about the route thence to Berlin, and, seeing that with Mainz as his only base he would form front to a flank, he transferred his line of communications to Forchheim—Würzburg Mannheim and Strasburg, all fortified depots as also Kronach. Another line ran Forchheim—Nürnberg Augsburg. The fortification of the depots economised communication troops and it is clear his line was safer than the Prussian. His retreat was arranged to be on the upper Danube at Ulm. Any Prussian raid across the lower Rhine would meet King Louis at Wesel and Mortier at Mainz—these two generals were to demonstrate as much as possible, but as a fact did little; King Louis had also orders to spread the report that 80,000 men would collect at Wesel, for Napoleon excelled in mystification. Measures were also concerted against any British raid on the French coast.

Prussia on the other side was on August 9, 1806, ignorant that the French Army was in South Germany and in this condition of ignorance issued mobilisation orders to the intense joy of the troops. The mobilisation was slow and unfortunately there were three commanders—the King, Brunswick and Hohenlohe. More unfortunately numerous Councils of War were held and in them Colonel von Massenbach displayed gross folly. As to plans there was much discussion—Hohenlohe wanted an offensive towards the Franken Wald which would have meant an attack on the French in front, Brunswick wanted to act via Fulda and cut Napoleon from the Rhine.

The result was a compromise, *i.e.*, Hohenlohe to manoeuvre *via* Hof, Brunswick *via* Erfurt. Then came the second and final plan, September 25, that Brunswick and Hohenlohe should pass through the Thuringian Wald on to Meiningen and Hildburghausen, interpose in the French centre at Schweinfurt and defeat the French wings in detail, for the Prussians did not know of Napoleon's concentration on Bamberg or of his altered line of communications. This plan assumed the French were all along the Main and would await attack and also involved the passage through the Thuringian Forest.

September 20 to 30 the Prussians held a 190-mile front— Right wing, 30,000, under Blücher and Rüchel from Paderborn through Hesse-Kassel to Eisenach; Centre, 55,000, at Naumburg; Left wing, 40,000, including the Saxons, under Hohenlohe at Zwickau, west of Chemnitz; Right and Centre were based on Berlin and the Elbe fortresses; Left on Dresden.

October 5 to 8 the front was reduced to 85 miles, *e.g.*, Blücher moved towards Eisenach south-eastwards, Centre moved to Erfurt, Left to Jena and Roda with advanced guard at Saalfeld and Tauentzien with 7,000 on the left front at Hof and Schleiz. Opposite this last general Napoleon had seven Army Corps on a front of thirty-eight miles, so that he could concentrate on his centre in one day and on either flank in two days.

Then again, October 4 to 7, came long Prussian Councils of War, condemned by Scharnhorst with his "It does not matter what you do in war, if you do it with strength," but on October 8 a report showed that the French were moving north-eastwards from Bamberg and that evening Brunswick renounced Plan No. 2 and issued orders that Hohenlohe should call Tauentzein to himself and concentrate with the main army west of the Saale between Rudolfstadt, Hochdorf, Blankenhain and Kahla, that the Duke of Weimar, commanding Advanced Guard of the main army towards the Thuringian Wald, should advance to Meiningen sending some cavalry on Schweinfurt, that Blücher and Rüchel should concentrate on Gotha and send detachments on Fulda to threaten enemy's communications, that Duke Eugene of Württemberg with the reserve, 16,000, should hurry from the too distant Magdeburg to Halle (this force illustrates the evil of a strategic reserve).

These orders for a concentration west of the Saale were sound except that Weimar's detachment and Blücher's detachment wasted 11,000 men, for they contained no enemy and occupied no strategic point. Detachments, though often necessary, should be kept as few as possible. Instances in this campaign are Weimar, Blücher and Ney round Magdeburg.

CHAPTER 5

Events to the Combat of Saalfeld, October 10

The French were executing the orders of September 19, the Guard travelling from Paris in carts and doing 260 miles in eight days.

These orders resulted in putting the French *corps d'armee* on October 3 along the upper Main from Würzburg with second line at Nürnberg and Amberg (Mortier however at Mainz), and on October 5 Napoleon at Würzburg issued fresh orders so as to cross the frontier the moment war should be declared.

THE FRENCH COLUMNS:

Right Wing—4th A.C., Soult, duke of Dalmatia, an able leader, 32,000 men and 48 guns;

6th A.C., Ney, duke of Elchingen, 20,000 men and 24 guns;

Bavarians, Wrede, 7,000 men and 18 guns: total 59,000 men and 90 guns.

Centre—1st A.C., Bernadotte, prince of Ponte Corvo, of great capacities, 20,000 men and 34 guns;

3rd A.C., Davout, second only to Masséna, 30,000 men and 44 guns;

Imperial Guard, 7,000 men and 36 guns;

Independent Cavalry, Murat, Grand Duke of Berg, 17,000 men and 30 guns: total, 74,000 and 144 guns.

Left Wing—5th A.C., Lannes, duke of Montebello, personal friend of the Emperor, 20,000 men and 28 guns; 7th A.C., Augereau, duke of Castiglione, of inferior capacities, 17,000 men and 36 guns: total, 37,000 and 64 guns.

Add to these Grouchy's 3,000 heavy cavalry (arrived October 14) and you get about 200,000 with 298 guns.

The orders of October 5 directed the Right to Baireuth (Prussian territory) on October 8 and thence to Hof, October 9; the Centre *via* Kronach, Lobenstein, Saalburg on October 9, and Schleiz; the Left, after a feint on Hildburghausen to mystify the enemy, *via* Coburg, Gräfenthal and Saalfeld on October 11 (really the 10th).

In the two Forests lateral communication was difficult and the left was the strategic flank and so Lannes screened that flank with cavalry. The centre was in advance and could support either wing. The Emperor did not early in the campaign launch forward his cavalry, mainly because he feared the renowned Prussian cavalry; in Berthier's despatch of October 7 Murat was directed to scout with light cavalry on the 8th in front of the centre and also to right and left.

October 8—The advance went on, Tauentzien retiring from Hof on Schleiz and some of his people being driven in a cavalry skirmish from Saalburg bridge. Besides Tauentzien there were on the right of the Saale 8,000 Saxons at Auma, a detachment at Neustadt and 600 cavalry at Pösneck.

October 9—A serious combat at Schleiz between Tauentzien and the leading troops of Murat and Bernadotte resulted in the French occupying Schleiz and in Tauentzien falling back on Auma.

The positions that night were:—

French—Left, Lannes at Gräfenthal and Augereau at Coburg;

Centre, Bernadotte at Saalburg-Schleiz and Davout at Lobenstein and Guard at Ebersdorf;

Right, Soult on Plauen, Ney in rear of Soult and Bavarians at Baireuth. The front was about 38 miles.

Allies (1) Hohenlohe had on the left of the Saale 8,000 men at Orlamünde and Prince Louis' advanced guard (8,000) at Rudolfstadt and Saalfeld; on the right of the Saale Tauentzien (7,000 and 8,000 Saxons) at Auma, detachment of 3,000 at Neustadt and 600 cavalry at Pösneck; (2) Main Army at Erfurt; (3) Weimar's advanced guard at Meiningen threatening Schweinfurt; (4) Rüchel near Gotha and Blücher at Eisenach with some troops on Fulda; (5) Reserve at Magdeburg. The front was ninety miles with three bodies out of reach.

October 10—Hamley writes:

On this day the Emperor wrote a letter to Soult from which we learn his view of the situation and it was an erroneous view. He believed that on the 5th Brunswick's army had moved towards Fulda and that Hohenlohe would try to advance through the Frankenwald. He inferred that Brunswick had moved so far that many days must elapse before he could rejoin Hohenlohe on the Saale. He believed that he would have only Hohenlohe to deal with and he imagined that general would concentrate on Jena.

.... and this was indeed Hohenlohe's and Massenbach's wish for the whole allied forces—it would mean frontal resistance to the French. The idea of Brunswick was to concentrate on the left bank, hence his order to Hohenlohe of the 8th of October to mass at Hochdorf. The two Headquarters hotly debated the question all the 9th of October, but Brunswick insisted on compliance. Which of these was the better plan? Clausewitz prefers a concentration on the left bank, because it was a flank position so threatening that Napoleon could not pass by it, he would also be very near the neutral Bohemian frontier, the left bank would confer great tactical advantages, Napoleon must form front to a flank whilst the Prussians would have all North Germany behind them—an excellent defensive position. A frontal defence is correct if you are very strong, otherwise adopt a strategic flank position.

Acting on his erroneous idea the Emperor at 8 a.m. issued orders for concentration, *i.e.*, Soult on Jena, Ney on Schleiz, Guard on Schleiz, Lannes and Augereau on Saalfeld, Murat, Bernadotte and Davout on Auma. Bavarians now under Prince Jerome Bonaparte to take Ney's place in second line to Soult. In other words he pivoted his left on Saale and swung round his right to cast its weight on Hohenlohe.

COMBAT OF SAALFELD

This town stood on the Saale connected by a bridge with Alten Saalfeld at the mouth of the Pösneck valley; steep hills lay to the west of the town and between them and the town was a steep glacis, crossed by the Siegenbach brook and by the ravine through Beulwitz, Crösten and Wolsdorf—both good cover.

Prince Louis with 8,300 Prussians and Saxons had his main force at Rudolfstadt; two battalions, half a battery and three squadrons at Saalfeld; a battery at Schwarza; Pelet's detachment of one battalion, one Jäger company, three squadrons and half a battery at Blankenburg. In the early morning the Prussian outposts were attacked, and at 9 a.m. the Prince brought up his main force from Rudolfstadt. He occupied a front from Crösten to Garnsdorf, facing west, Beulwitz feebly held.

Mr. Petre, upon whose Conquest of Prussia I chiefly depend for this combat, remarks upon the errors of the Prince, namely, his right was *en l'air* and he had the defile of the Saalfeld bridge behind him, and Bonnal in his *Rosbach to Jena* specially criticises the weak occupation of Beulwitz.

About 10 a.m. Suchet's Division of Lannes' Army Corps with the light cavalry approached Garnsdorf; placing some troops near this village and protected by swarms of skirmishers the mass of the division made for the woods on the upper part of the glacis with the idea of outflanking the Prince's right, cutting his retreat and driving him into the river. The Prince realising this at 11 a.m. took the following measures—he sent one Prussian battalion to Schwarza and another to the Sandberg, connecting the last with himself by placing a battalion between Aue and Crösten. He then had an important message from Hohenlohe.

Up to 11 a.m. Prince Louis' idea was that Hohenlohe from Orlamünde would cross the Saale for Auma and that the main army would follow and that he was to cover this flank movement of Hohfenlohe from the French Left. Therefore he rightly held Saalfeld, says Mr. Petre, but Colonel Maude says "wrongly" as distance alone would have sufficiently covered this flank movement of Hohenlohe But at 11 a.m. he had a verbal message that Hohenlohe wished him to stop at Rudolfstadt and not attack the enemy and that he (Hohenlohe) would this day have his Headquarters at Kahla. It is clear that the Prince should now have broken off the action at Saalfeld, but, says Houssaye, he was impetuous. Donaldson, *Military History and Modern Warfare*, puts it thus:

Hohenlohe was from the Councils of War aware of Brunswick's intention to move, after concentration, to the right bank of the Saale. He accordingly delayed bringing his troops to the left bank because he thought they would only have to recross. This seems understandable, but Brunswick peremptorily ordered him to cross. This necessitated the Prince stopping at Saalfeld to cover the operation. The same writer also argues that the Prince should have retired, not owing to the message, but owing to the tactical development of the action. Alison holds that the Prince stood firm at Saalfeld in order to cover the evacuation of the magazines there.

The French skirmishers had by this time taken Beulwitz and when six Saxon battalions from the Prince's centre moved forward in *échelons*, in the Great Frederick's style, to deliver an attack, the French fire from Beulwitz proved too much and the Saxons fell back followed by the French skirmishers who captured Crösten, but at 12 noon a Saxon counter-attack recarried Crösten. At 1 p.m. a French counter-attack retook the place.

All this time the leading French Droops making for the Sandberg were debouching through Aue; they drove the Prussian battalion off the Sandberg and their cavalry cut up the connecting battalion between Aue and Crösten. Seeing all this and his left driven over the Saalfeld bridge, the Prince headed a charge of five squadrons in his centre against the French 9th and 10th Hussars and in it he was killed in single combat with the hussar Guindey. The pursuit was vigorous; Prussians and Saxons escaped across the Saale, whilst others including the battalion at Schwarza were driven by cavalry as far as Rudolfstadt.

During the combat we note the inaction of Pelet at Blankenburg; the French cavalry returning from Rudolfstadt moved against him, as did French infantry from Unter Wirbach. Pelet at once retired *via* Stadt Ilm and Blankenhain, reaching Weimar on October 12.

The allies lost 2,000 men and thirty-three guns, the French lost 172 men out of 14,000 in action. The moral effect was great especially on the Saxons. Note Lannes' initiative in reaching Saalfeld a day sooner than ordered, an act which success alone excused, and Augereau's want of initiative in waiting at Coburg for fresh instructions.

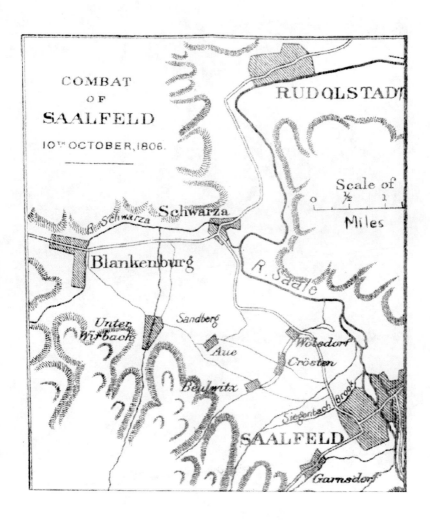

COMBAT
OF
SAALFELD
10ᵀᴴ OCTOBER, 1806.

RUDOLSTADT

Scale of
0   ½   1
Miles

B. Schwarza

Schwarza

Blankenburg

R. Saale

Unter
Wirbach

Sandberg

Aue

Wölsdorf

Crösten

Beulwitz

Siegenbach Brook

SAALFELD

Garnsdorf

CHAPTER 6

Operations Leading to Jena
and Auerstedt

October 10, evening positions:—
French Right Wing—Soult at Plauen, Ney at Gefell, west of Plauen, Bavarians in rear.

Centre—Bernadotte near Auma with Murat in front, Davout and Guard at Schleiz, heavy cavalry under Grouchy in rear.

Left Wing—Lannes at Saalfeld and Augereau on Gäafenthal.

Allies, Hohenlohe's main force at Kahla whither were moving all his men still east of the Saale; Main Army at Blankenhain; Rüchel at Erfurt; Blücher at Gotha, still with troops threatening Fulda; Weimar's advanced guard at Meiningen threatening Schweinfurt. At 10 p.m. orders issued for concentration—Hohenlohe on the front Jena—Kapellendorf; rest at Weimar. This was the fifth Prussian plan and purely defensive.

October 11—At night the allies stood thus:—
Main Army, Rüchel and Blücher at Weimar, Hohenlohe at Jena where a grave panic occurred. There were still troops near Fulda but the Duke of Weimar was retiring and the Reserve under Eugene of Württemberg was at Halle. The same night the French faced north—Left Wing, Lannes at Neustadt, Augereau at Saalf eld; Centre, Bernadotte at Gera supporting Murat, Davout and Guard at Auma; Right Wing, Soult at Weida and Ney at Schleiz. "The army was thus massed between the Elster and the Saale cutting the Saxons from Dresden and capturing much

baggage " (Hamley). This was a strategic deployment for a battle at Gera with one error, *i.e.,* the isolation of Augereau (compare Mortier at Dürrenstein, 1805). At this juncture Napoleon's new view as to the enemy called for new arrangements.

Very late this night the French Monarch formed a new idea as to Prussian movements—they were massing not on Gera but all on Erfurt (really on Weimar) and the battle would be on the 16th (really on the 14th). This new idea arose from the statements of prisoners captured by the light cavalry near Gera that the King was at Erfurt with 200,000 men and Murat confirmed this (Maude). He must now wheel round and face westwards and in doing so decided to seize the important point of Naumburg, not with the right who were farther off, but with the centre; this would make the right the centre and *vice versâ* and might lead to confusion and Prince Kraft calls it an error though there was no confusion.

The change did not affect the Guard or the Heavy Cavalry. He issued the necessary orders.

October 12—Bernadotte marched from Gera for Naumburg, Davout from Auma for the same place; this, the new right, had Murat with light cavalry in front as far as Leipzig. The new centre had Soult at Gera, Ney at Auma, Emperor and Guard at Gera, heavy cavalry and Bavarians in rear.

On the left Lannes from Neustadt recrossed the Saale at Kahla for Jena, Augereau crossing at Saalfeld and passing through Pösneck swung round after Lannes and recrossed the Saale at Kahla—this *détour* caused by late arrival of order. At 2 p.m. Lannes collided with Hohenlohe's outposts at Göschwitz and drove them through Winzerla; this success being helped by a flanking detachment sent by Lannes down the right bank which crossed at the Burgau bridge. Lannes reached Winzerla with Augereau behind him, both on the left bank and both exposed to the mass of the enemy, for Napoleon thought Erfurt, not Weimar, was their point of assemblement.

This day the allies, except Weimar and the Fulda troops and the Reserve, were on the front Weimar—Jena, with outposts on the Saale between Jena and Camburg, in no good heart and with supplies in an unsatisfactory state.

CHAPTER 7

Battle of Jena, October 13 & 14

October 13—Davout captured the allies' depot, Naumburg, with its great stores and there came upon some retreating pontoon trains; and the Emperor then directed Ney from Auma to Roda, Bernadotte to Naumburg to join Davout and that Auma should be arranged as a temporary base. But at 9 a.m. he wrote to Murat "The veil is rent (*Enfin, le voile est déchiré*); the enemy retreats on Magdeburg or is on the point of attacking Lannes" and at once issued orders. Murat with the light cavalry and Bernadotte were ordered back to Dornburg, Soult and Ney called up to Jena as also the Guard and the heavy cavalry—the fact is he had not expected battle till the 16th.

As to Lannes, he from Winzerla moving in a fog approached Jena, north of which place lies the Landgrafenberg up which goes a steep road from Jena and on the top of which is the so-called Napoleonsberg or Windknolle. Note the road from Weimar and the Mühl Thal alongside it. Lannes easily occupied Jena and pushing up the Landgrafenberg his skirmishers forced back Tauentzien's advanced guard on to Lützeroda—Closewitz. As the fog rose Lannes standing on the Windknolle saw 40,000 men in front and his own peril, but Massenbach saved him.

That officer had at Weimar heard Brunswick's latest plan—the Duke foolishly rejected the idea of awaiting the enemy with all his forces behind the Saale. He was situated like Wellington at Salamanca, 1812, and a victory would have saved him. Instead he divided his forces by choosing the following plan, moved to do so partly by the news that Naumburg had fallen—the main army under the King (for the Court and the Queen accompanied the army) and himself and with Blücher leading the cavalry was to move this day, the 13th, left of the Ilm, cross the Unstrutt River at Freyburg, join the Reserve from Halle and make for Magdeburg; the Saale would cover the strategic flank especially if the Kösen defile were held. Rüchel would stop at Weimar for the Duke of Weimar, and then both follow Brunswick.

Hohenlohe would with his 38,000 men between Weimar and Jena act as a rearguard. Massenbach was so impressed with Hohenlohe's defensive *rôle* that on rejoining that Prince he effectually stopped him from crushing Lannes. Colonel Maude however, and Houssaye, state that Massenbach carried a precise message from the Duke that no serious engagement with the enemy was to be undertaken. In effect Hohenlohe then took post between Isserstedt and Kapellendorf, facing south, Tauentzien still holding Lützeroda and Closewitz on high ground called Dornberg, even higher than the Windknolle.

The Prince's notion was that he would be attacked from the south only by Lannes and Augereau and that the main body of Napoleon was on Dresden or Leipzig—Brunswick had the same idea. For this reason Hohenlohe did not occupy Jena at all or the Landgrafenberg in strength. Besides he supposed the French could not ascend the Landgrafenberg by the path that Lannes took. This day the Saxons in want of food threatened to desert and Hohenlohe had to take the extraordinary (as it then seemed) step of allowing them to requisition.

On the French side Napoleon at 4 p.m. joined Lannes on the Landgrafenberg. "Hohenlohe's Army was visible, but Rüchel at Weimar was hidden as was Brunswick's Army marching for Kösen" (Hamley). Napoleon wrongly judged he had all the Prussians in his front, whilst himself having in hand only Lannes' Army Corps and the Guard infantry. He saw his danger, especially as the artillery column got jammed in the narrow path up the Landgrafenberg; in person he removed the difficulty. That night he kept visiting the outposts and called to Jena *via* Dornburg Murat and his light horsemen. Baron Marbot states that a Saxon *curé* guided Lannes up the hill and Colonel Maude says the French stood on it during the night "close-packed" and that the thick mist of the morning of October 14 alone saved this mass and the Emperor from annihilation by the Prussian guns (compare the unlucky fog at; Spion Kop in the Boer War).

This day, the 13th, the positions in detail were—Hohenlohe's main body, 25,000 men, faced the Weimar road between the *Schnecke* or winding road and Kapellendorf, his left, 8,000 men, under Tauentzien at Closewitz and Lützeroda on the Dornberg. Hearing a false rumour that the enemy was coming *via* Camburg and Dornburg, Hohenlohe posted General Holtzendorf, 5,000 men, on the tableland above so as to close those issues. The total number of guns with the above was 12½ batteries.

On the other side Lannes' 5th Army Corps had its left, Gazan's division, near Kospeda and its right, Suchet's division, close in front of Closewitz; on the Windknolle the Guard infantry; total 24,000 infantry, 1,500 cavalry and forty-two guns. Augereau from Kahla stood south of the Mühl Thal and west of Jena. Ney, Soult and the heavy cavalry were hurrying up, but Davout and Bernadotte were far off—this no doubt Napoleon regretted but it turned out fortunately.

The Emperor's orders for battle issued during the night:— Augereau on the left to cross the Mühl Thal and move *via* Kospeda, keeping a force south, of the Mühl Thal moving level with himself; in the centre, moving against Tauentzien, Lannes, Guard, Ney (with precise order to move on Lannes' right) and Murat with light cavalry; on the right Soult *via* Löbstedt and the Rauh Thal. Troops would have light infantry in front and then two lines; Guard and heavy cavalry in reserve. "What is important is to deploy on the plain and the enemy must be driven from the positions necessary for our deployment." As to Davout and Bernadotte they were to come on the left rear of the enemy at Apolda.

October 14—At 6 a.m. there was a very thick mist and in it Lannes advanced preceded by skirmishers. In the mist his corps

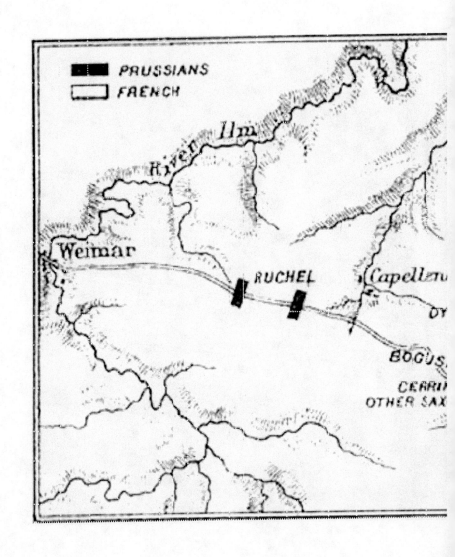

BATTLE OF
JENA
14 Oct. 1806
10 a.m.

0   1   2 Miles

Apolda

Dornburg

Nerkwitz

ST HILAIRE

STOLZENDORF

SOULT

dorf

Vierzehn Heiligen

GRAWERT

Closewitz

HERM

CAVALRY

NEY

SUCHET

NAPOLEON

AUSKI
TA
NS

COSPUNBE

GAZAN

GUARD

Löbstädt

R. Saal

AUTEREAU

NEY

Landgrafenberg

Mühlbach

MURAT

JENA

bent towards Closewitz and thus a gap arose between him and Augereau, which gap Napoleon filled with twenty-five guns, partly Guard guns. Suchet's division however carried the Closewitz wood and Closewitz itself, whilst Gazen's division captured Lützeroda, 7.45 a.m., fog then clearing these villages should have been strongly held by Tauentzien. Meantime Soult on the right with his leading division (St. Hilaire) came in two columns from Löbstedt—left column up the Rauh Thal, right column *via* Zwätzen. The left column repulsed Tauentzien's extreme left on Hermstedt; and on the left Augereau, Desjardins' division leading, *via* Kospeda made for Isserstedt. The object of these first onsets by Napoleon was to gain space upon the plateau for deployment.

Hohenlohe, at last convinced of a serious French attack, directed Tauentzien to fall back so as to occupy a front from the heights above the *Schnecke* to Klein Romstedt. At 9 a.m. Tauentzien retired, followed by Lannes' divisions, Gazan on the left and Suchet on the right; these divisions though they took twenty-four (Houssaye says 12) guns in their advance towards Krippendorf and Vierzehnheiligen, which villages the Prussians foolishly evacuated, could do no more and halted, for as yet, 9.15 a.m., there was arrived only Ney with his advanced guard on the left of Marshal Lannes: Soult had not come up and Holtzendorf marching to the cannon appeared on Suchet's right. He had assembled at Rödigen and at 10 a.m. he advanced on Krippendorf, but just at that moment St. Hilaire occupied the woods west of Rodigen this forced Holtzendorf into a retreat on Stobra, a retreat fiercely harassed by Soult's light cavalry. Holtzendorf reached Stobra 11.30 a.m. (and Apolda at 2 p.m.). Soult pursued only as far as Nerkwitz and then pivoted towards Alt Gönna and Krippendorf.

At this time, 11 a. m , Lannes stood between Krippendorf and Vierzehnheiligen, facing west, and on his left stood Ney's advanced guard and then came the twenty-five guns. More to the left east and south-east of Isserstedt, came Augereau's divisions tinder Desjardins and Heudelet; in reserve between Lützeroda and Krippendorf the Guard. As to the enemy Holtzendorf was on Stobra and Hohenlohe himself facing the French held a front through Isserstedt and Vierzehnheiligen.

In this battle Ney showed great initiative and Bonnal in his *Jena* says he forced Napoleon into fighting this day; the original orders had been that Ney should come up on Lannes' right; perhaps, as Mr. Petre suggests, the Emperor modified these orders when he saw the gap between Lannes and Augereau. What Bonnal refers to occurred now—the Emperor, having gained space for deployment and ignorant of what had happened to Soult, would have suspended the combat, but Ney with his advanced guard—four battalions and a brigade of light cavalry—delivered an attack with his cavalry south of Vierzehnheiligen which was answered by charges of the Prussian squadrons. These were repulsed by Ney's infantry in squares with the help of Lannes' hussars (see Maude) and that Marshal's infantry moving forward captured Vierzehnheiligen. Then arrived Ney's main body and some heavy cavalry.

Hohenlohe's infantry (Grawert's division) just west of Vierzehnheiligen began to form line for attack, as if in the barrack square, within reach of the French fire, though "fortunately for them the Emperor's big battery could not touch them as a roll in the ground intervened" (Maude). The French skirmishers skilled in cover severely punished their close formations and sheltered by garden walls themselves suffered little from the Prussian volley fire. What rendered it worse for the Prussians was that the village of Vierzehnheiligen was occupied by the French and attack of villages formed no part of the duties of the Prussian line troops—it was the duty of the Fusiliers. I cannot do better than quote Colonel Maude:

> At short musket range the leading *échelon* was halted and line formed upon it with accuracy. Each battalion opened fire by company volleys as its dressing was completed, whilst a howitzer battery set the houses on fire.

Hohenlohe should at once have assailed the village, but he

waited for Rüchel. This contest lasted two hours, 11 a.m. to 1 p.m., and Hohenlohe tried with cavalry to envelop Lannes' right but in that quarter arrived 1.15 p.m. St. Hilaire's division of Soult's Army Corps and the put Hohenlohe's left in danger. Meantime on his right Augereau had carried Isserstedt near which the 7th Chasseurs charged the Saxon cavalry, 12.30 p.m.

ARRIVAL OF GENERAL RÜCHEL

At Weimar at 9 a.m. an appeal from Hohenlohe had reached Rüchel and leaving there a small force to meet the Duke of Weimar he rightly responded to the appeal by starting from Weimar with 15,000 men at 10 a.m., but for unknown reasons not till 2 p.m. did he reach Kapellendorf. All this time Hohenlohe's men were getting demoralised, at least in the left and centre and on them the French Sovereign unleashed his mass of horsemen. The pursuit was undertaken by Murat, carrying in bitter contempt a riding whip, with the light cavalry of Lannes, Ney and Augereau; behind came the heavy cavalry and some dragoons, whilst on the French right and north of Vierzehnheiligen Soult's light cavalry acted.

The flight and the pursuit led to the valley of Kapellendorf, where the victorious cavalry saw fresh Prussian troops pushing through the disordered fugitives—it was Rüchel at last. Massenbach had met Rüchel and urged on him this offensive action through Kapellendorf—it would have been far better to hold a defensive position till evening. Both Hohenlohe and Rüchel acted as befits German generals, and Rüchel's cavalry repulsed Soult's light horsemen and "with the steadiness of the parade ground his infantry marched up the hill from Kapellendorf to Gross Romstedt in *échelons* of two battalions each, the centre leading" (Petre)—Maude puts it "in *échelons* of three battalions each, from the centre."

Met by overwhelming fire from Soult, Lannes, Ney and Desjardins' division, charged by cavalry and quite outnumbered they broke and the whole force fled on Weimar, Rüchel falling. So much for Hohenlohe's left and centre.

As to his right near the *Schnecke, i.e.*, Zeschwitz I's Saxons, it had been posted in order to cover the Prussian right, but the corps of Augereau passing through Kospeda had left Zeschwitz both undisturbed and useless. About 11 a.m. Hohenlohe directed him to take the offensive the moment Grawert's infantry got into alignment with him, but as this never happened he remained motionless till after Rüchel had been routed. The French Emperor having ascertained there was this isolated body behind his left, sent against it one of Ney's divisions, and *Heudelet's* division moving on both sides of the Mühl Thal, and some cavalry regiments.

The above is Houssaye's account of the fighting against Zeschwitz, but Colonel Maude and Mr. Petre consider that Zeschwitz had been far earlier assailed by Heudelet moving on both sides of the Mühl Thal, and that Augereau's other division (Desjardins) when at 12 noon it gained Isserstedt had fallen on the Saxons' left flank. However that may be, the Saxons retired towards Kapellendorf, 3 p.m., now in French hands after Rüchel's defeat and were consequently charged by dragoons and heavy cavalry on all sides—6,000 surrendered to Murat, but Zeschwitz I with 300 horse cut through to Hohlstedt "where he met his brother, Zeschwitz II, who still held the Saxon cavalry together" (Petre).

They then took post between Frankendorf and Umpferstedt trying to stop the pursuit, but Murat's cavalry drove them over the Ilm at Denstedt, whilst the remnant of Rüchel crossed at Ulrichshalben. At 4 p.m. near Weimar some of the allies made a last effort and then fled to Weimar.

In this battle 53,000 allies had opposed 96,000 French and the former were now a rabble, except Holtzendorf who, pressed by Bernadotte at Apolda, had passed the Ilm at Ulrichshalben 3 p.m. The allies lost 12,000 killed and wounded, 15,000 prisoners and many guns, French lost between 4,000 and 6,500 men. As to cavalry the Prussians had 10,500 against 8,000, but cavalry did not succeed against the French infantry.

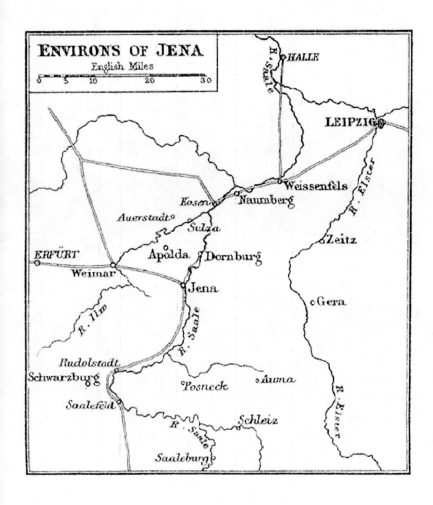

ENVIRONS OF JENA

English Miles

0   5   10   20   30

HALLE

R. Saale

LEIPZIG

R. Elster

Weissenfels

Kosen

Naumberg

Auerstadt

Sulza

Zeitz

ERFÜRT

Apolda

Dornburg

Weimar

Jena

R. Saale

R. Ilm

Gera

Rudolstadt

Schwarzburg

Auma

Posneck

R. Elster

Saalefeld

Schleiz

R. Saale

Saaleburg

Jena was won by strategy, tactics had little to do with it, *e.g.*, in this battle and Auerstedt the Prussians were compelled to form front to a flank and the Saxons were quite intercepted; the results of a defeat in such a position are obvious.

Napoleon fought with a defile in his rear; is this a dangerous course? There is no doubt that if all the allies had opposed him at Jena he might have found the defile a serious evil. It is not easy to lay down a rule on this matter, as the cases are conflicting, *e.g.*, at Fredericksburg, 1862, the Federals got off easily and at Friedland, 1807, the Russians were ruined, in each case lighting on the bank of a river. If one must lay down a rule it would seem that if there is enough space between the battle front and the defile to arrange your retreat before you reach the defile, it is not dangerous and *vice versâ*.

Note Napoleon's use of twenty-five massed guns; this massing of guns became his practice afterwards as at Friedland, 1807. As the French expected Davout they delivered no great flank attack, though Soult's action may be regarded as such.

Courses open to Hohenlohe:—

(1) His best plan was to have attacked Lannes on October 13;

(2) If he had occupied in strength the front Isserstedt—Rauh Thal he might have stopped Napoleon from deploying;

(3) Col. Maude suggests that he might have called up Rüchel and early on the 14th have fallen back on Brunswick's Army and together they might have crushed Davout.

Note the Prussians' barrack square tactics at Vierzehnheiligen and their failure to arrange for a retreat. When Rüchel came up he should have covered the retreat and not tried offensive action at all.

If Napoleon's orders for Jena had been carried out they would have led to concentration on the battle field as was the case with the allies at Waterloo, 1815—an interior line general like Napoleon concentrates before the battle, an exterior line general like Moltke concentrates on the battlefield. Napoleon unwillingly adopted this plan because he had to fight sooner than he expected. He exceptionally concentrated on the battle field at Eylau, 1807, and at Bautzen, 1813.

CHAPTER 8

Battle of Auerstedt, October 14

On October 13th the main Prussian army marched from Weimar, *via* Umpferstedt, and crossed the Ilm between Wickerstedt and Mattstedt expecting to join the Reserve from Halle under Duke Eugene, but bivouacked at night at Auerstedt without seizing the defile of Kösen over the Saale though they knew the French were at Naumburg—nay, Davout took this defile in the night, October 13 to 14. Schmettau with the leading Prussian division reached Gernstedt and the whole force totalled 39,000 infantry, 9,000 cavalry and 230 guns against Davout's 25,000 infantry, 1,400 cavalry and 44 guns, but his were veteran troops. As a fact Bernadotte might have helped Davout but he even withdrew Sahuc's dragoon division.

On October 13 in the afternoon the Emperor's orders to Davout and Bernadotte were that if they heard an attack on Lannes they were to manoeuvre to their left to his aid; further orders reached Davout at 3 a.m. on the 14th directing him from Naumburg and Kösen on Apolda, so ignorant of Brunswick's march was Napoleon, but already on the evening of the 13th Davout's cavalry reconnoitring had met Prussian mounted men near Hassenhausen and a prisoner told him Brunswick was approaching.

October 14, the Battle—In the early morning in a dense mist Gudin's division passed the Kösen bridge, preceded by some *chasseurs* who riding through Hassenhausen fell on Blücher with 600 cavalry near Poppel—the French cavalry were repulsed on their infantry at Hassenhausen. Blücher then fell under fire from artillery and skirmishers and after losing five of his eight horse guns moved to his left, whilst Schmettau was arriving through Poppel. At 8 a.m. full on Gudin's right, formed in squares at Hassenhausen, came Blücher with 1,100 *cuirassiers*, dragoons and hussars; Gudin formed his men in battalion squares, chessboard fashion, and opposed to the torrents of horse, the fire of three ranks, and the points of their bayonets; in person Davout encouraged his men, there was no need, says Houssaye:—"*Ces hommes sont résolus et ardents*," Not a square broke. The infantry fire and that of a battery told heavily, but Blücher charged repeatedly; finally the arrival of the leading troops of Friant's division caused the Prussian cavalry to break away towards Speilberg 8.30 a.m., which was lucky as Schmettau's division was threatening Gudin's front.

At 9 a.m. Schmettau with Wartensleben's division on his right arrived, whilst on the French side Friant's whole division moved to Gudin's right and towards Spielberg—Gudin's skirmishers using cover punished Schmettau, whilst Friant helped by Davout's only cavalry (Vialannes' three light cavalry regiments) captured Spielberg and approaching Poppel threatened Schmettau's left rear. At this time, 10 a.m., Gudin's left, south of Hassenhausen, was hard pressed by Wartensleben's superior numbers and though the French general had repulsed Schmettau on his right, had killed Schmettau himself and the Duke of Brunswick, yet it was only by holding fast to Hassenhausen, his *point d'appui* (compare Vierzehnheiligen at Jena—probably the Prussians should have attacked these two villages with the bayonet), that he saved himself, for Wartensleben was turning his left and, besides, Orange's division had arrived not only to connect Wartensleben with Schmettau, but also to protect the latter's left flank against Friant.

Wartensleben too had with him numerous reserve cavalry under Prince William. At this crisis, 11 a.m., arrived along the road from Kösen to Hassenhausen Morand's division which hotly assailed Wartensleben and was in turn charged by Prince

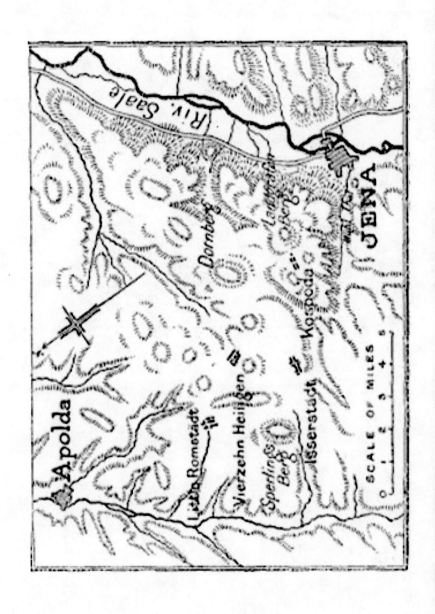

Riv. Saale

Dornberg

Landgrafenberg

Kospoda

Closewitz

JENA

Apolda

Rodigen

Rometadt

Vierzehn Heiligen

Sperling's Berg

Isserstadt

SCALE OF MILES
0 1 2 3 4 5

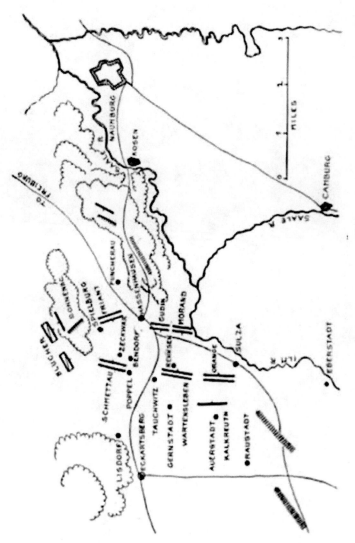

BATTLE OF AUERSTEDT

William—the cavalry were not well led, the French formed battalion squares, chessboard fashion, and repulsed them with cries
of "*Vive l'Empereur!*" Davout now passed from the defensive to
the offensive.

Morand assailed Wartensleben in spite of an attempt of part
of Kalkreuth's Prussian reserve to circle round Morand's left. Finally Morand gained the right flank of Schmettau and half Orange's division fighting west of Hassenhausen. Meantime Friant
had in spite of half Orange's division seized Poppel, capturing
1,000 men, and sent part of his force on Lisdorf.

About 12 noon Morand and Friant threatening the enemy's
flanks, Gudin drove their centre through Taugwitz and in spite
of the able efforts of Kalkreuth (this is the impression left on
my mind after reading Mr. Petre's *Conquest of Prussia*, but Colonel Maude, states Kalkreuth sent forward his reserve in driblets,
though admitting the King was partly responsible) with the rest
of his reserve near Gernstedt, the converging onslaught of the
three French divisions was too much for him and the whole
Prussian army fled *via* Eckartsberga and thence part through
Buttstädt and part through Mattstedt and Buttelstedt. (Houssaye
makes Brunswick's army flee on Apolda and there meet Hohenlohe's fugitives). Luckily for the Prussians Davout had few
cavalry—his infantry pursued to Eckartsberga and his three light
cavalry regiments to Buttstädt. The Prussians lost 10,000 killed
and wounded and 3,000 prisoners and nearly all their guns; the
French lost 7,000 men.

Tactical Comments on Auerstedt:

The conduct of Bernadotte was peculiar. We know that at 3
a.m., October 14, Davout had an order to move from Naumburg and Kösen on the left rear of the enemy at Apolda; this
order went on "If the Prince of Ponte Corvo, *i.e.*, Bernadotte,
is with you, you can march together, but the Emperor hopes
he will be at Dornburg." At 4 a.m. Bernadotte had this order at
Naumburg and, ignoring the first part, marched up to Dornburg
which he reached 11 a.m., October 14. He should have reached

Dornburg sooner, but as he had not started when he got the order he should have gone with Davout—as a fact he gave no help in either battle, and all he did was to close the Dornburg passage, though Houssaye represents him as coming *via* Carnburg. The Marshal was selfish and jealous and acted as he did in spite of Davout 's offer to serve under him; Prince Kraft holds that he was one who preferred manoeuvring to battle—see his conduct at Wagram, 1809 (Donaldson). Alison exceptionally holds that Bernadotte did right, "If the Prussians had escaped by Dornburg what could he have said."

This battle was an "*affaire de rencontre*" in which both sides had to form under fire. This explains much, *e.g.* the absence of any arrangements for retreat. Davout, though inferior in numbers, executed a double flank attack; his seizure of the Kösen defile allowed him to debouch upon the *plateau* whereas the Prussians were hampered by the difficulty they experienced in deploying. When Kalkreuth held Gernstedt the Prussians, says Houssaye, were still superior in numbers and if the King had not been affected by Brunswick's death and by the repulse of his renowned cavalry he might have renewed the battle with success.

In both battles note that modern rifles would have prevented cavalry charges against infantry; note also the close order of the Prussians, their omission to take cover, the control exercised by generals, the clumsy method of loading and firing and the short range.

CHAPTER 9

The Pursuit, the Battle of Halle and the Entry into Berlin, October 15 to 27

On the night after the battle Napoleon instead of retiring to rest sat up dictating orders for the pursuit, though he did not get Davout's report till 9 a.m. on the 15th. This pursuit was a strategic pursuit as was that after Waterloo, 1815.

At night, October 14 to 15, Lannes, Augereau, Ney and the Guard were at Weimar, Soult on Ulrichshalben, Bernadotte on Apolda, and Davout at Eckartsberga. As to the Prussians, their main army from Eckartsberga had fled partly *via* Buttstädt and partly *via* Buttelstedt, whilst Hohenlohe's troops fled on Buttelstedt joining the others, all in panic. On October 15 the King collected some of the main army at Sömmerda, Hohenlohe's forces making for Weissensee and Sondershausen. Of all their forces only two bodies remained effective

(1) the Reserve at Halle,

(2) the Duke of Weimar's detachment which as it retired from the Thuringian Forest heard of the Jena battle and made for Erfurt.

The French Sovereign conciliated Saxony by liberating the Saxon prisoners of war and ultimately Saxony, whose Elector was raised by Napoleon to the Kingly rank, became a firm ally of France. He also issued orders arranging not for a direct or a lateral pursuit but for what we may call a radiating pursuit—Davout to rest at Naumburg, Lannes and Augereau to rest at Weimar; Ney from Weimar on Erfurt, Soult from Ulrichshalben on Buttelstedt, Bernadotte from Apolda to cross the Ilm with Halle as his objective, thus cutting off the line of retreat from Weimar to Naumburg and shutting out the enemy from the great road to Magdeburg; half the Reserve, *i.e.* Independent Cavalry with Murat on Erfurt, the other half with Soult.

On the French Left this day, the 15th, Murat approached Erfurt and in spite of the efforts of the Duke of Weimar to withdraw the 10,000 Prussians and Saxons in the town, they all capitulated to the French cavalry leader. Soon afterwards Ney reached Erfurt. The capitulation of Erfurt was disgraceful. The Duke of Weimar then started for Langensalza and thence, joined by the Fulda troops, October 16, on to Mülhausen, 12,000 strong. The same day Murat and Ney reached Langensalza, lost all trace of Weimar and turned towards Soult.

That marshal, October 15 and 16, made for Buttelstedt and in his front was the King retreating from Sömmerda on Sondershausen with his troops cut in half by the French Klein's dragoons and Lasalle's marvellous light cavalry at Weissensee—thus the Prussian rearguard under Kalkreuth and Blücher was between Soult and Klein. Negotiations between Klein and Kalkreuth followed of which each side gives a different account but, whatever the truth, Klein agreed to give Kalkreuth a free passage—was he to blame? He was no doubt weak and had succeeded in delaying the enemy. The French allege and the Prussians deny that Blücher falsely stated that an armistice was concluded. Soult however having come up through Weissensee drove Kalkreuth and Blücher north through Sondershausen on Nordhausen;

Next day, October 17, Soult reaching Nordhausen attacked Kalkreuth, whose object was to reach Magdeburg *via* the Harz Mountains and Halberstadt; Hohenlohe now in chief command had already passed through the last place, the roads were horrible and the troops starving and demoralised. To ease the march

Blücher with the heavy artillery, went off from Nordhausen right round on the town of Brunswick to cross the Elbe at Sandau, north of Magdeburg. All this day Murat and Ney were rapidly moving from Langensalza straight on Nordhausen. Goltz suggests that instead of retiring into Magdeburg Hohenlohe should have burst out westwards, joined Blücher, the Duke of Weimar and General Lecoq at Hameln on the Weser and drawn the French in that direction and thus have given the King and his Russian allies time: Massenbach opposed this plan.

On the French Right, October 16 and 17, Davout at Naumburg, Lannes and the Guard from Weimar to Naumburg, Augereau from Weimar to Auerstedt; Bernadotte moved on Querfurt for Halle where was the Prussian reserve under Duke Eugene, 16,000 strong. On the 17th in the Battle of Halle Bernadotte attacked this force driving it on Dessau on the Elbe. It fled across that river and on October 19 reached Magdeburg with half its original strength. Duke Eugene should not have fought, but should have retired and held the line of the Elbe, covering Berlin.

On October 18 Napoleon transferred his communications to a new line, namely, Mainz—Fulda—Eisenach—Erfurt—this line was better than the original one and after Jena the Elector of Hesse Kassel would not think of damaging it; on this new line points were fortified and provisioned. It is said that a modern invading general cannot change his line of communications unless he has command of the sea,

The Emperor had now to deal with the fact that the enemy was trying to concentrate on Magdeburg. On this date, October 18, the French stood thus: on the right Bernadotte and Lannes (from Naumburg) at Halle, Augereau from Auerstedt at Merseburg, Davout from Naumburg at Leipzig; on the left Soult, Murat, and Ney moving from Nordhausen through the Harz Mountains after Hohenlohe and shepherding the Prussians into the "mousetrap" of Magdeburg.

On the 19th the French Left pressed on *via* Halberstadt and Quedlinburg; and the Emperor then moved his Right so as to be able to concentrate and also to secure the passage of the Elbe—therefore Lannes on Dessau, Davout on Wittenberg and Bernadotte ready to march left of the Saale towards Magdeburg to reinforce the left wing, whilst at Halle ready for emergencies stood the Guard, Augereau, and the just arrived heavy cavalry of Grouchy. It is obvious that the heavy cavalry was slow, the fact is that its horses had been used up by the light cavalry. At the same date Hohenlohe and Kalkreuth were between Halberstadt, Quedlinburg and Magdeburg where was the remnant of the Reserve; Blücher and the Duke of Weimar sweeping round on the town of Brunswick.

During the next two days, October 20 and 21, the French Left—Murat, Soult and Ney—arrived at Magdeburg where were Hohenlohe and the Reserve and where confusion reigned, the place being stacked up with wagon-trains, but Kalkreuth had broken off to pass the Elbe lower down. As to the French Right Davout seized the bridge of Wittenberg and crossed, Lannes mastered that of Dessau, but Bernadotte was in the Emperor's opinion dilatory in securing a passage at Barby. At this period both armies suffered much and resorted to pillage and rapine, though the French had organised a line of communications from Erfurt through Naumburg, Leipzig, Wittenberg, and ultimately to Berlin; at Wittenberg, which was fortified, a bakery and an arsenal were established and also at Erfurt in case of retreat—so careful was the Emperor.

He had first intended to surround Magdeburg, but by October 22 .he altered his mind and decided to leave Soult and Ney to deal with the fortress and to move the rest on Berlin; therefore crossing the Elbe above Magdeburg mainly at Dessau and Wittenberg there marched for the Prussian capital Lannes, Augereau, Murat, Davout, Grouchy's heavy cavalry (Becker commanding *vice* Grouchy sick), Imperial Guard, and Bernadotte who had struggled across at Barby.

Soult and Ney invested Magdeburg on the left bank, but meantime, *i.e.*, on October 21 Hohenlohe with 24,000 men had fled from the city north-eastwards meaning to reach the Oder and joined on the way by the troops of Kalkreuth, now under Hirschfeld. The direct route to the Oder at Cüstrin could not be taken because Napoleon was too near it. Magdeburg was left with 25,000 garrison, too many but the men would not leave.

October 23 the French Monarch announced that all Prussia west of the Elbe was annexed and his right wing continued its move on Berlin—Davout close to the city and at Potsdam, Lannes, Guard, Heavy Cavalry and Augereau. On October 25 Davout rightly entered the city first and two days later the Emperor in person. (Incidents of Prince Hatzfeldt and Pastor Ehrmann). He had not marched with his troops in the tremendous distances some of them covered, but he had to arrange everything, to carry on a vast correspondence not only with his officers but with his statesmen and with foreign governments, and with an eye to effect took every opportunity to pay reverence to the memory of the great Frederick. Financial questions were pressing and he levied immense contributions, compelled all Prussian civil authorities to swear fealty to himself and issued an ordinance for the civil organisation and military occupation of the whole country.

All this time the French had lost all trace of the Duke of Weimar and Blücher. As a fact those two generals had met and passing round by the town of Brunswick Blücher crossed the Elbe at Sandau October 24 and the Duke following managed to impose upon Soult who tried to cut him off from the river, and on October 26 also crossed the river at Sandau and was at once superseded by Winning. The reason of this supersession was that Napoleon would not allow him to be neutral as Duke of Weimar and yet hostile as a Prussian general, especially as the French ruler had promised the Duchess to respect the Duchy—the same course was pursued with reference to the Duke of Brunswick. Soult therefore wanted to cross the Elbe below Magdeburg and to leave Ney to deal with the fortress.

During these days, October 21 to 24, Hohenlohe with troops unskilled in requisitioning and passing through a level and poor country moved west of the town of Brandenburg with Stettin as his objective—he was joined on his march by Blücher who took over the rearguard. All these days Bernadotte, "the link between Napoleon and Ney" (Petre), was slowly approaching the town of Brandenburg.

CHAPTER 10

The Surrender of Hohenlohe

Acting now in a region covered by rivers, canals and lakes Hohenlohe in order to reach Stettin proposed that Blücher should protect his right rear and wait for the Duke of Weimar (who did not cross at Sandau till October 26) and that another force should hold all the passages over the canalised waters that stretch from Sandau on the Elbe eastwards through Oranienburg to Oderberg on the Oder, but already the Emperor had captured Spandau and informed by Bernadotte of Hohenlohe's direction had launched Murat and Lannes in pursuit and had seized "the all-important passage of Oranienburg" (Petre) on the River Havel.

On October 26 the French cavalry routed Hohenlohe's covering force (the force that should have held the canal passages) at Zehdenick on the Havel and drove it on Stettin. This French success forced Hohenlohe into the eccentric route *via* Fürstenberg, for Murat and Lannes were hurrying along the Zehdenick-Prenzlau road.

On October 27 Hohenlohe advanced from Fürstenberg towards Prenzlau where were supply depots, and Murat followed by Lannes pressed on the same place; collisions occurred between Murat and Hohenlohe's advanced guard and the latter general seeing he could not hope to get into the main Zehdenick-Prenzlau road decided to move eccentrically through Schönermark. He reached that place October 28 with starving troops and again wasted time in deliberations. Then the move on Prenzlau began again and on the same place pressed Murat's starving cavalry followed by the intrepid Lannes' advanced guard. In the result Hohenlohe just arrived first and at once received a French officer, Captain Hugues, bearing a flag of truce—this officer boldly stated that French troops in large numbers surrounded Prenzlau, and Hohenlohe sent Colonel Massenbach back with him to Prince Murat to see if it was true; immediately afterwards Murat's cavalry attacked Prenzlau. The attack succeeded in carrying the town but only a few of Lannes' infantry had arrived and Murat's whole force was far inferior to Hohenlohe. The latter indeed could have still got to Stettin.

Meantime however Massenbach had been to Murat and had been led to think that 100,000 French troops surrounded Prenzlau. Hohenlohe was still against surrender when Murat requested a personal interview and categorically stated that lie had 100,000 men. The result was that Hohenlohe, having lost all the Prenzlau supplies and being short of ammunition and convinced that both his flanks were turned, surrendered to the Grand Duke of Berg on October 28, 1806. This disgraceful surrender disposed of 13,000 Prussians and 89 guns.

Murat's leading cavalry, Lasalle's marvellous light brigade, then hurried on to Stettin and on October 29 summoned the place and though the governor had a garrison of 5,000 and ample stores he yielded, perhaps blinded by Lasalle's assertion that 40,000 French were at hand! A shameful surrender and Napoleon wrote to Murat:—

> My compliments on the capture of Stettin; if your light cavalry take fortified towns, I must disband my engineers and melt down my heavy artillery.

On November 1 Cüstrin on the Oder surrendered to Davout's advanced guard. This advanced guard consisted of a regiment of foot and two guns, whilst the governor of Cüstrin had 90 guns mounted and 400 in arsenal, 4,000 troops and everything necessary for a long siege. The besiegers could not take possession till the garrison furnished them with boats.

All up to the Oder was in the conqueror's hands except Blücher, Winning, and the places of Magdeburg, Hameln, Hesse-Kassel and Hamburg, Of these Magdeburg was soon to fall; Ney with 18,000 men had been left to invest this place which had a garrison of 25,000, but no sooner did Kleist, the governor, hear of the Prenzlau surrender, than he capitulated, November 8.

CHAPTER 11

The Last Efforts of Blücher

Ney having taken over the siege of Magdeburg, Soult was, as he desired, allowed by the Emperor to cross the Elbe in pursuit of Winning—he did this on October 28 at Tangermünde and at once made for Wittstock, through which place Winning had already passed. Soult selected this route because he foresaw Blücher's doubling back to the Elbe. At the same time Bernadotte marching through the town of Brandenburg reached Fürstenberg on the same day as Soult crossed the Elbe, and, assuming that Blücher would try to reach the Oder *via* Pasewalk he followed north-eastwards, but hearing that Blücher had swung north-westwards through Neu Strelitz he followed in the same direction through Neu Brandenburg and Ankershagen. Blücher had reached Boitzenburg when he heard of the Prenzlau surrender and though in the midst of the enemy he and Scharnhorst took the bold course—double back and join Winning. The operations now run through the territory of the Duke of Mecklenburg till they reach the Free City of Lübeck.

The result was that on October 30 the combatants stood thus: Murat and Lannes at Stettin, Bernadotte on Neu Strelitz, Soult on Wittstock, Blücher and Winning (22,000 strong) in connexion west of Neu Strelitz pursued by 50,000 French, *i.e.*, Bernadotte, Soult, and Murat who swept round from Stettin north of Neu Strelitz.

Mr. Petre thus describes Blücher's plan:—

Winning had wished to march for Rostock, then to embark and pass by sea beyond the Oder. This scheme Blücher disapproved; his object was to keep back from the Oder as many of the French as possible, so as to give time for the Russians and Prussians to organise behind that river and to call in the Silesian troops (compare Stonewall Jackson's action in the Valley in 1862). He decided therefore to try to reach the Elbe near Lauenburg and to cross it there and then either move on Magdeburg or join Lecoq's troops in Hanover,

..... and act against the French communications, but we shall see that "pressed in rear by Bernadotte and cut by Soult from the Elbe and by Murat from the Baltic he was hemmed in upon the neutral Free City of Lübeck." (Hamley).

Goltz considers that Blücher would now have done well to strike a heavy blow at Bernadotte, but he was overpersuaded and on November 1 retired along the road to Schwerin hotly pursued by Soult and Bernadotte and severe rearguard actions marked the movement, Colonel Yorck (afterwards so famous) greatly distinguishing himself.

Next day, November 2, Blücher continued his retirement and the French followed, Soult on the left, Bernadotte in the centre, Murat on the right, but they lost contact.

Next day, November 3, contact was regained and again rearguard actions took place, in the course of which Bernadotte was nearly captured. The Prussians crossed the River Stoer at the Fähre Bridge just south of Schwerin. Both here and at Strelitz even Blücher never dreamt of requisitioning supplies. During all this Murat had been on the right of Bernadotte sweeping the country almost as far as the sea, but he was now drawing down on Schwerin from the north-east, as Bernadotte approached it from the east and Soult from the south-east.

Blücher then altered his plan for three reasons:

(1) exhaustion of his men and shortage of supplies and artillery ammunition,

(2) the French had mastered the Fähre Bridge,

(3) a report, erroneous indeed but very unlucky for the Prussians, that Soult interposed between Lauenburg and Schwerin.

The new plan was to retire on the neutral Free City of Lübeck, a place full of resources, and at that moment there were some Swedish troops there. The fact is that Blücher not only overestimated the French numbers but also imagined that Bernadotte was in his front, and Murat and Soult on either flank. On November 4 the new movement began, Soult in pursuit merely crossing the Stoer south of Schwerin, Bernadotte merely passing through that town and Murat merely arriving at it.

On November 5 Blücher fell back close to Lübeck finding the 1,800 Swedes already embarked but detained by the wind in the Trave below Lübeck; the French followed, Bernadotte coming east of Lübeck, Murat south-east and Soult south of the place. Blücher himself requested of the Senate supplies and ammunition, promising to retire from the city, if attacked. Supplies he got but no ammunition and regardless of his promise prepared the city for defence, for he was aware that he stood almost on the neutral frontier of Denmark.

On November 6 the French columns simultaneously attacked Lübeck, Bernadotte capturing many Swedes on transports in the River Trave (he treated them well, hence his future election as Crown Prince of Sweden). The defence and the assault were equally desperate; in the end the French succeeded and Blücher left by the western gate and then turned north towards Ratkau. He had no right to involve a neutral city in the horrors of an assault—and the horrors were fearful.

On November 7 Blücher reached Ratkau, enclosed between the Danish frontier, the Trave and the sea and this day his 7,000 men surrendered to the 35,000 pursuers; the celebrated Scharnhorst shared in Blücher's surrender.

"The expedition of Blücher," says Goltz, "failed because it involved a contradiction in terms. It was conceived in the spirit of the Thirty Years' War, when armies traversed Germany from end to end. But to do this troops must know how to live on the country and that Blücher's troops did not think of doing. That being the case it would have been better to have attacked Bernadotte at the outset."

The Emperor has now in my account made a clean sweep up to the Oder except of Silesia, Hamburg, Hesse-Kassel and Hameln. The few Prussians left in the lower Rhine under Lecoq had retired into Hameln on the Weser when they heard of the Jena battle, whilst Napoleon moved forward King Louis of Holland from Wesel and Mortier from Mainz so as to converge on the town of Kassel. The intention was to punish the Elector of Hesse-Kassel who though nominally neutral was fiercely anti-French. On November 1 accordingly the two French generals entered Kassel whence the Elector fled. Mortier then dealt with Hanover, Hameln and Hamburg, whilst Prince Jerome's Bavarians passing through Saxony entered Silesia and besieged the strong places.

CHAPTER 12

General Comments

Hamley remarks that this campaign presents both armies forming front to a flank—at first this is true of the French only so long as Mainz was their base, it is true of the Saxons but not of the Prussians; at Jena and Auerstedt however it is true of both Prussians and French whilst the Saxons were then absolutely intercepted. It is obvious from this campaign that when an army forms front to a flank defeat means ruin, victory means safety—compare Salamanca, 1812. The two battles opened to Napoleon a route to Berlin shorter than any route the Prussians controlled.

The Napoleonic system employed a Strategic Advanced Guard to gain information, to give the main army time and space to manoeuvre, and to fix the enemy—this was very necessary when the main body moved in a *carré stratégique* because a strategic square must have time for concentration or for deployment. This strategic advanced guard marched close behind the cavalry screen; it first appeared in 1800 in North Italy and was completed in 1806. The Napoleonic strategic advanced guard was composed of the three arms; the Great Frederick's strategic advanced guard was composed of cavalry only.

In the French system the supreme command will not decide till after the engagement of the strategic advanced guard, in the German system it will decide after the engagement of the cavalry—hence French gain in certainty, Germans gain in time. In 1806 when the Grand Army crossed the Frankenwald it had as strategic advanced guard three light brigades and two divisions of dragoons and Bernadotte's army corps, all under Murat.

With regard to cavalry the Army Review, July, 1911, remarks that Napoleon sent forward for reconnaissance only a part of his mounted men; he objected to an independent campaign of cavalry masses in advance of the army.

Colonel du Cane in his *Campaigns in Alsace*, says:—

An example of the combination of the main cavalry force with a strong force of infantry as an advanced guard occurs in the Jena campaign. During the advance in the celebrated battalion-square, Oct. 8 to 14, Murat's cavalry and Bernadotte's corps formed the advanced guard. Bernadotte, under Murat's orders, was half a day's march in front of Davout, whilst the cavalry was only a little ahead of Bernadotte. It was not till Oct. 13 that this advanced guard was broken up and it was Lannes, not Murat, who located Hohenlohe's army at Jena on Oct. 13, the cavalry reconnoitring to the north having discovered nothing.

Why did Napoleon restrict his cavalry to the right bank of the Saale and keep them so supported by infantry? Because he was afraid of the Prussian horsemen. In any case instructions to his cavalry to seek out the enemy's main force would have agreed better with modern views. As such instructions would have taken the cavalry to the left of the Saale there would have been risk in supporting them with infantry, as was proved by the danger of Lannes and Augerau when separated from the rest of the army by the Saale, Oct, 12 and 13.

On this matter of the danger of the two marshals it was part of Napoleon's system to consider that the destruction of any unit was a mere nothing, provided it assisted his general scheme. Colonel Maude says:

Napoleon aimed at economy of force, that is, human life, on the whole transaction and provided he was successful in this the fate of a detachment did not worry him.

As to this I should remark the authorities differ as to the routes taken by Lannes, and Augereau:

(1) Lannes in my account crosses the Saale at Saalfeld, then *via* Neustadt, then recrosses the Saale at Kahla and goes to Jena by the left bank; others say he crossed at Saalfeld and then moved *via* Neustadt on Jena by the right bank;

(2) Augereau in my account crosses the Saale at Saalfeld, then *via* Pösneck recrosses the Saale at Kahla and on to Jena by the left bank; others say he moved from Saalfeld to Jena entirely by the left bank.

Jomini thus describes Napoleon's system:

. . . . . he aimed to destroy the hostile army; to detect the relative advantages presented by different zones of operation; to concentrate on the most suitable one; to ascertain the position of the enemy; to fall like lightning upon his centre, if his front was too extended; or upon his strategic flank; to outflank him; to cut his line; to pursue him to the last—such was Napoleon's system.

(*The Art of War* by Jomini also published by Leonaur.)

Note Napoleon's *carré stratégique* or *bataillon carré*, that is battalion square of 200,000 men ready to unite for battle in 48 hours; during the advance on the upper Saale he kept his army "massed in a space of 40 miles by 40 miles so as to be able to form front in any direction" (James, *Modern Strategy*) and up to the battles he generally arranged two wings and a strong central reserve; and it will be noted that he made himself stronger at Jena than at Naumburg. This was not only because he supposed all the enemy was at Jena, but also because a defeat at Jena would be more fatal to him than a defeat at Naumburg. Jena was the decisive point and therefore Napoleon massed his main force there and even if Davout had been defeated, Napoleon would afterwards have beaten Brunswick.

Contrast with this the scattered position of the allies who on October 9 held a front of 90 miles. The Prussian plan (No. 2) of September 24 to 25 involved a passage through the difficult Thuringian Forest with its consequent separation. That this plan was superseded by the third plan (October 8), *i.e.*, a concentration west of the Saale in a defensive flank position is an illustration of the truth of Hamley's principle that "when two armies are manoeuvring against each other's flanks or communications, that army whose flank or communications are most immediately threatened will abandon the initiative and conform to the movements of its adversary" (compare Novara, 1849, and Salamanca, 1812).

The fact is that, as Donaldson says, Prussian unreadiness and the desirability of waiting for the Tsar rendered defensive strategy preferable and some go so far as to allege that the Prussians should have retired on to the Oder River. Donaldson in *Military History and Modern Warfare* remarks that Napoleon considered Prussia had three possible courses of action:—

(1) Concentrate behind the Elbe;

(2) Concentrate at Eisenach and advance on Mainz;

(3) Concentrate on the upper Saale.

Brunswick's cardinal error lay in not waiting entrenched behind the Elbe and a defective strategic concentration can hardly ever be repaired except by a genius or by a lucky victory. It must be admitted that stopping behind the Elbe meant sacrificing Hesse—Kassel and Saxony, but as a fact the Elector of Hesse—Kassel did nothing and Prussia was full of the Great Frederick's offensive spirit. It would have made a great difference if the great depot of Naumburg had been fortified; and if Brunswick had stopped united at Jena, Napoleon would have fought all the enemy with a defile in his rear.

A feature of this campaign is the ease with which the fortresses surrendered—they should have resisted more sternly and Napoleon said that if Berlin had been fortified the Prussians could have waited there for the Russians.

In almost all theatres there are what are called strategic points, *i.e.* points the possession of which confers an advantage and of such points Gera, a knot of roads, is in this case an example.

Waterloo and Jena were followed by great strategic pursuits, but it is obvious that no such pursuits marked the campaigns of 1870 and 1904 when, instead of a strategic pursuit, we find a new plan and a systematic advance. The reasons for this are according to Goltz the exhaustion and dispersal of the troops, the range of the enemy's guns and feelings of humanity. Rapid pursuit after battle is far less common than one would suppose; it is not easy to launch your cavalry after battle, *e.g.*, Johnston failed to pursue after Bull Run, 1861. In this pursuit there was remarkable marching, *e g.*, Bernadotte did 375 miles in twenty-three days and Murat passed from Jena to Stettin, Lübeck and Warsaw—850 miles in six weeks.

As to Hohenlohe's retreat from Magdeburg, it was retarded from the necessity of spreading to procure food, but he did not take the shortest route, he placed much cavalry on his left flank (compare MacMahon in 1870), he lost time by quartering his men in the villages each day, for "no one dared set custom at defiance by requisitioning supplies and enforcing close billets" (Goltz). But for these errors he could have reached Stettin, and in any case he was wrong in surrendering.

Prussia underrated her enemy and held the notion that war was a game of chess between Kings in which the people must not suffer, *e.g.*, Kleist surrendered to save Magdeburg and at Cüstrin the governor said "Reduce the town to ashes! That I cannot do." In fact the military spirit was lacking and people thought they could win by art without bloodshed; is Germany passing now through a similar phase? (Goltz).

Alison writes—

Such was the astonishing campaign of Jena; Europe had hardly recovered the shock arising from the fall of Austria in 1805, when she beheld Prussia's overthrow by the shock of Jena. Without pausing in their career of conquest the French troops had marched from the Rhine to the Oder; the fabric of the Great Frederick had fallen by a single blow and a Great Power was obliterated. There were

Oberndorf
Hermstedt
Klein-
Romstedt
Groß-
Krippend
B
Vierzehn-
Sperlingsbg.
heiligen
Kapellendorf
Kötsenm
Isserstedt
Litzeroda
Hohlstedt
Sächs. Truppen un:
Gen. Zeschwitz
Kospe

Korps d. Marsch
Korps d. Oudinots
Korps d. Preuß. Armee un: Hoh.
Korps d. Lugo aux
Korps
Korps

☐ Preußen
⬚ Sachsen } Verbündete
☐ Franzosen

Gefechtsmomente:

A · Angriff der Franzosen auf die fr. Avantgarde
B · Treffen der Hauptarmeen
C · Zurückwerfen des Rüchelschen Korps.

Maßstab 1: 100 000

0   1   2   Kilometer

captured in seven weeks 350 standards, 4,000 guns, six fortresses, 80,000 prisoners; on the Vistula remained only 15,000 men to the King of Prussia. The talents displayed by Napoleon in this campaign, though of a high order, were not equal to the transcendent abilities evinced in 1805.

Doubtless the celerity with which the hazardous advance of the Duke of Brunswick across the Thuringian Forest was turned to the best account, the vigour of the fight at Jena and the incomparable pursuit are worthy of the highest admiration. But in the outset of the campaign he ran unnecessary risk and but for a change in the position of the bulk of the Prussian army, of which he was ignorant, might have been involved in as great a catastrophe as the rout on the banks of the Inn (1800) had been to the Austrians. To advance and attack the Prussian army, strongly posted at Jena, through the narrow and rugged defiles of the Landgrafenberg, was a greater piece of military rashness than it was in the Archduke John to advance against Moreau through the pines of Hohenlinden.

Napoleon himself said:—

The first principle of the military art is never to fight with a defile in your rear.

Had the whole Prussian army continued posted at the opening of the defiles, the French could never have debouched. It was incorrect to oppose 80,000 men to 40,000 at Jena, whilst leaving 30,000 to meet 60,000 at Auerstedt, but the truth is the French Sovereign deemed himself invincible; up to 1806 his principle had been to fight in favourable conditions, after 1806 in any conditions rashness that was to lead to Moscow, 1812, and Leipzig, 1813. He thus wrote at Potsdam on October 25:—

J'ai écrasé la monarchie Prussienne, j'écraserai les Russes s'ils arrivent; je ne crains pas les Autrichiens.

The real reason for the Prussian *débacle*, in spite of the popular enthusiasm for the war, was not the rout of Jena but the fact that the monarchy, newly cemented by the genius of the Great Frederick, had not had the time to acquire a general patriotic feeling—compare the immense result of the single battle of Hastings, 1066.

Great was the enthusiasm of France and the despondency of the rest of Europe; all coalitions against France had failed, Austria backed by British gold and by Russian legions had sunk in the conflict and now the Great Frederick's splendid army had been scattered.

It seemed as if Europe must for years be enslaved by the conquering nation, and few took the view of old Blücher that the time would come when Europe in a body would rise in arms against the dreaded conqueror. It was true and Germany taught in the school of adversity rose in the War of Liberation, 1813.

THE SUPPLY SYSTEM:—

Though the French Army was splendid it was, now actuated more by pillage than by patriotism, *e.g.*, after Jena, Marshal Soult had to check his troops' rapine, and plundering was not confined to the privates. In the Prussian army, an army purely professional and so hide-bound that even during its flight from Jena all the routine forms were observed, looting was unknown, for the Great Frederick's supply system depended on magazines, not on requisitions. On the other hand Napoleon held that war must support war and though he collected "great depots of stores as a reserve at central points, his armies as a rule lived by requisition. When they had to pass through a poor tract the Emperor insisted on their carrying sufficient food to carry them beyond it. Thus the French soldiers were adepts at extracting food" (Petre).

The French success in 1806 as in other years was largely due to the fact that as against the ultra-methodical supply system of the Great Frederick, they seized at once on requisitions carrying on themselves only bread and brandy and then after a victory established a regular "line." The French were skilled marauders and sucked nutriment out of the ground, where others starved—but theirs was regulated requisition. The allies had the old-fashioned cumbrous system of the Great Frederick, dependent on magazines and fatal to mobility; they did not know how to requisition. Goltz says the Prussians, afraid of the civil law, would not seize food and thus left it for the enemy. Napoleon on the other hand marched ahead of his wagons and his men when passing through the Frankenwald carried four days' bread and biscuit and after crossing the Saale had to rely on requisitions.

He established, as was his custom, a temporary base at Auma, and his system, not indeed pillage but regulated requisition, gave him mobility and worked well in fertile countries and successful campaigns. His maxim "*War must support war*" meant an organised system, not a rude quartering of troops on the people in fact he was most careful in organising communications in 1806.

The old system of the Great Frederick met the new system directed by Napoleon and was shattered and at the root of this new system lay the new supply system (Hamley).

The Prussian Army, old-fashioned and entirely dependent on its magazines and quite unable, like the Austrian, to live on the country, had enormous impedimenta and was very sensitive about its line of communications. This fact was the base of Napoleon's plans in 1800, 1805 and 1806.

The French Army on the contrary lived on the country and could therefore march rapidly but on the approach of battle it was necessary to revert to the system of magazines which were formed by the grand parks, requisitions on the country and the magazines of the enemy. In this campaign Napoleon had two lines of communication—

(1) Mannheim to Forchheim,

(2) Augsburg (south of the Danube) to Forchheim.

On bursting into Saxony and partly uncovering those communications and with a battle imminent, he checked for a mo-

ment his rear convoys and lived on a centre of operations—
Auma—where he collected his parks of artillery, bread, meal,
and set up hospitals. What Auma was in this case, Piacenza was in
1800, and Augsburg in 1805 (Anderson, *Great Campaigns, 1796-
1815*).

Mr. Petre remarks on the fact that the Prussian soldier relying
on his commissariat would throw away the rations he carried
whereas the Frenchman would keep it for an emergency.

LEONAUR

ALSO FROM LEONAUR
AVAILABLE IN SOFTCOVER OR HARDCOVER WITH DUST JACKET

THE 2ND MAORI WAR: 1860-1861 *by Robert Carey*—The Second Maori War, or First Taranaki War, one more bloody instalment of the conflicts between European settlers and the indigenous Maori people.

A JOURNAL OF THE SECOND SIKH WAR *by Daniel A. Sandford*—The Experiences of an Ensign of the 2nd Bengal European Regiment During the Campaign in the Punjab, India, 1848-49.

THE LIGHT INFANTRY OFFICER *by John H. Cooke*—The Experiences of an Officer of the 43rd Light Infantry in America During the War of 1812.

BUSHVELDT CARBINEERS *by George Witton*—The War Against the Boers in South Africa and the 'Breaker' Morant Incident.

LAKE'S CAMPAIGNS IN INDIA *by Hugh Pearse*—The Second Anglo Maratha War, 1803-1807.

BRITAIN IN AFGHANISTAN 1: THE FIRST AFGHAN WAR 1839-42 *by Archibald Forbes*—From invasion to destruction-a British military disaster.

BRITAIN IN AFGHANISTAN 2: THE SECOND AFGHAN WAR 1878-80 *by Archibald Forbes*—This is the history of the Second Afghan War-another episode of British military history typified by savagery, massacre, siege and battles.

UP AMONG THE PANDIES *by Vivian Dering Majendie*—Experiences of a British Officer on Campaign During the Indian Mutiny, 1857-1858.

MUTINY: 1857 *by James Humphries*—Authentic Voices from the Indian Mutiny-First Hand Accounts of Battles, Sieges and Personal Hardships.

BLOW THE BUGLE, DRAW THE SWORD *by W. H. G. Kingston*—The Wars, Campaigns, Regiments and Soldiers of the British & Indian Armies During the Victorian Era, 1839-1898.

WAR BEYOND THE DRAGON PAGODA *by Major J. J. Snodgrass*—A Personal Narrative of the First Anglo-Burmese War 1824 - 1826.

THE HERO OF ALIWAL *by James Humphries*—The Campaigns of Sir Harry Smith in India, 1843-1846, During the Gwalior War & the First Sikh War.

ALL FOR A SHILLING A DAY *by Donald F. Featherstone*—The story of H.M. 16th, the Queen's Lancers During the first Sikh War 1845-1846.

LEONAUR

ALSO FROM LEONAUR
AVAILABLE IN SOFTCOVER OR HARDCOVER WITH DUST JACKET

AT THEM WITH THE BAYONET *by Donald F. Featherstone*—The first Anglo-Sikh War 1845-1846.

STEPHEN CRANE'S BATTLES *by Stephen Crane*—Nine Decisive Battles Recounted by the Author of 'The Red Badge of Courage'.

THE GURKHA WAR *by H. T. Prinsep*—The Anglo-Nepalese Conflict in North East India 1814-1816.

FIRE & BLOOD *by G. R. Gleig*—The burning of Washington & the battle of New Orleans, 1814, through the eyes of a young British soldier.

SOUND ADVANCE! *by Joseph Anderson*—Experiences of an officer of HM 50th regiment in Australia, Burma & the Gwalior war.

THE CAMPAIGN OF THE INDUS *by Thomas Holdsworth*—Experiences of a British Officer of the 2nd (Queen's Royal) Regiment in the Campaign to Place Shah Shuja on the Throne of Afghanistan 1838 - 1840.

WITH THE MADRAS EUROPEAN REGIMENT IN BURMA *by John Butler*—The Experiences of an Officer of the Honourable East India Company's Army During the First Anglo-Burmese War 1824 - 1826.

IN ZULULAND WITH THE BRITISH ARMY *by Charles L. Norris-Newman*—The Anglo-Zulu war of 1879 through the first-hand experiences of a special correspondent.

BESIEGED IN LUCKNOW *by Martin Richard Gubbins*—The first Anglo-Sikh War 1845-1846.

A TIGER ON HORSEBACK *by L. March Phillips*—The Experiences of a Trooper & Officer of Rimington's Guides - The Tigers - during the Anglo-Boer war 1899 - 1902.

SEPOYS, SIEGE & STORM *by Charles John Griffiths*—The Experiences of a young officer of H.M.'s 61st Regiment at Ferozepore, Delhi ridge and at the fall of Delhi during the Indian mutiny 1857.

CAMPAIGNING IN ZULULAND *by W. E. Montague*—Experiences on campaign during the Zulu war of 1879 with the 94th Regiment.

THE STORY OF THE GUIDES *by G.J. Younghusband*—The Exploits of the Soldiers of the famous Indian Army Regiment from the northwest frontier 1847 - 1900.

LEONAUR

ALSO FROM LEONAUR

AVAILABLE IN SOFTCOVER OR HARDCOVER WITH DUST JACKET

OFFICERS & GENTLEMEN *by Peter Hawker & William Graham*—Two Accounts of British Officers During the Peninsula War: Officer of Light Dragoons by Peter Hawker & Campaign in Portugal and Spain by William Graham .

THE WALCHEREN EXPEDITION *by Anonymous*—The Experiences of a British Officer of the 81st Regt. During the Campaign in the Low Countries of 1809.

LADIES OF WATERLOO *by Charlotte A. Eaton, Magdalene de Lancey & Juana Smith*—The Experiences of Three Women During the Campaign of 1815: Waterloo Days by Charlotte A. Eaton, A Week at Waterloo by Magdalene de Lancey & Juana's Story by Juana Smith.

JOURNAL OF AN OFFICER IN THE KING'S GERMAN LEGION *by John Frederick Hering*—Recollections of Campaigning During the Napoleonic Wars.

JOURNAL OF AN ARMY SURGEON IN THE PENINSULAR WAR *by Charles Boutflower*—The Recollections of a British Army Medical Man on Campaign During the Napoleonic Wars.

ON CAMPAIGN WITH MOORE AND WELLINGTON *by Anthony Hamilton*—The Experiences of a Soldier of the 43rd Regiment During the Peninsular War.

THE ROAD TO AUSTERLITZ *by R. G. Burton*—Napoleon's Campaign of 1805.

SOLDIERS OF NAPOLEON *by A. J. Doisy De Villargennes & Arthur Chuquet*—The Experiences of the Men of the French First Empire: Under the Eagles by A. J. Doisy De Villargennes & Voices of 1812 by Arthur Chuquet .

INVASION OF FRANCE, 1814 *by F. W. O. Maycock*—The Final Battles of the Napoleonic First Empire.

LEIPZIG—A CONFLICT OF TITANS *by Frederic Shoberl*—A Personal Experience of the 'Battle of the Nations' During the Napoleonic Wars, October 14th-19th, 1813.

SLASHERS *by Charles Cadell*—The Campaigns of the 28th Regiment of Foot During the Napoleonic Wars by a Serving Officer.

BATTLE IMPERIAL *by Charles William Vane*—The Campaigns in Germany & France for the Defeat of Napoleon 1813-1814.

SWIFT & BOLD *by Gibbes Rigaud*—The 60th Rifles During the Peninsula War.

LEONAUR

ALSO FROM LEONAUR
AVAILABLE IN SOFTCOVER OR HARDCOVER WITH DUST JACKET

ADVENTURES OF A YOUNG RIFLEMAN *by Johann Christian Maempel*—The Experiences of a Saxon in the French & British Armies During the Napoleonic Wars.

THE HUSSAR *by Norbert Landsheit & G. R. Gleig*—A German Cavalryman in British Service Throughout the Napoleonic Wars.

RECOLLECTIONS OF THE PENINSULA *by Moyle Sherer*—An Officer of the 34th Regiment of Foot—'The Cumberland Gentlemen'—on Campaign Against Napoleon's French Army in Spain.

MARINE OF REVOLUTION & CONSULATE *by Moreau de Jonnès*—The Recollections of a French Soldier of the Revolutionary Wars 1791-1804.

GENTLEMEN IN RED *by John Dobbs & Robert Knowles*—Two Accounts of British Infantry Officers During the Peninsular War Recollections of an Old 52nd Man by John Dobbs An Officer of Fusiliers by Robert Knowles.

CORPORAL BROWN'S CAMPAIGNS IN THE LOW COUNTRIES *by Robert Brown*—Recollections of a Coldstream Guard in the Early Campaigns Against Revolutionary France 1793-1795.

THE 7TH (QUEENS OWN) HUSSARS: Volume 2—1793-1815 *by C. R. B. Barrett*—During the Campaigns in the Low Countries & the Peninsula and Waterloo Campaigns of the Napoleonic Wars. Volume 2: 1793-1815.

THE MARENGO CAMPAIGN 1800 *by Herbert H. Sargent*—The Victory that Completed the Austrian Defeat in Italy.

DONALDSON OF THE 94TH—SCOTS BRIGADE *by Joseph Donaldson*—The Recollections of a Soldier During the Peninsula & South of France Campaigns of the Napoleonic Wars.

A CONSCRIPT FOR EMPIRE *by Philippe as told to Johann Christian Maempel*—The Experiences of a Young German Conscript During the Napoleonic Wars.

JOURNAL OF THE CAMPAIGN OF 1815 *by Alexander Cavalié Mercer*—The Experiences of an Officer of the Royal Horse Artillery During the Waterloo Campaign.

NAPOLEON'S CAMPAIGNS IN POLAND 1806-7 *by Robert Wilson*—The campaign in Poland from the Russian side of the conflict.

LEONAUR

ALSO FROM LEONAUR
AVAILABLE IN SOFTCOVER OR HARDCOVER WITH DUST JACKET

OMPTEDA OF THE KING'S GERMAN LEGION *by Christian von Ompteda*—A Hanoverian Officer on Campaign Against Napoleon.

LIEUTENANT SIMMONS OF THE 95TH (RIFLES) *by George Simmons*—Recollections of the Peninsula, South of France & Waterloo Campaigns of the Napoleonic Wars.

A HORSEMAN FOR THE EMPEROR *by Jean Baptiste Gazzola*—A Cavalryman of Napoleon's Army on Campaign Throughout the Napoleonic Wars.

SERGEANT LAWRENCE *by William Lawrence*—With the 40th Regt. of Foot in South America, the Peninsular War & at Waterloo.

CAMPAIGNS WITH THE FIELD TRAIN *by Richard D. Henegan*—Experiences of a British Officer During the Peninsula and Waterloo Campaigns of the Napoleonic Wars.

CAVALRY SURGEON *by S. D. Broughton*—On Campaign Against Napoleon in the Peninsula & South of France During the Napoleonic Wars 1812-1814.

MEN OF THE RIFLES *by Thomas Knight, Henry Curling & Jonathan Leach*—The Reminiscences of Thomas Knight of the 95th (Rifles) by Thomas Knight, Henry Curling's Anecdotes by Henry Curling & The Field Services of the Rifle Brigade from its Formation to Waterloo by Jonathan Leach.

THE ULM CAMPAIGN 1805 *by F. N. Maude*—Napoleon and the Defeat of the Austrian Army During the 'War of the Third Coalition'.

SOLDIERING WITH THE 'DIVISION' *by Thomas Garrety*—The Military Experiences of an Infantryman of the 43rd Regiment During the Napoleonic Wars.

SERGEANT MORRIS OF THE 73RD FOOT *by Thomas Morris*—The Experiences of a British Infantryman During the Napoleonic Wars-Including Campaigns in Germany and at Waterloo.

A VOICE FROM WATERLOO *by Edward Cotton*—The Personal Experiences of a British Cavalryman Who Became a Battlefield Guide and Authority on the Campaign of 1815.

NAPOLEON AND HIS MARSHALS *by J. T. Headley*—The Men of the First Empire.

LEONAUR

ALSO FROM LEONAUR
AVAILABLE IN SOFTCOVER OR HARDCOVER WITH DUST JACKET

COLBORNE: A SINGULAR TALENT FOR WAR *by John Colborne*—The Napoleonic Wars Career of One of Wellington's Most Highly Valued Officers in Egypt, Holland, Italy, the Peninsula and at Waterloo.

NAPOLEON'S RUSSIAN CAMPAIGN *by Philippe Henri de Segur*—The Invasion, Battles and Retreat by an Aide-de-Camp on the Emperor's Staff.

WITH THE LIGHT DIVISION *by John H. Cooke*—The Experiences of an Officer of the 43rd Light Infantry in the Peninsula and South of France During the Napoleonic Wars.

WELLINGTON AND THE PYRENEES CAMPAIGN VOLUME I: FROM VITORIA TO THE BIDASSOA *by F. C. Beatson*—The final phase of the campaign in the Iberian Peninsula.

WELLINGTON AND THE INVASION OF FRANCE VOLUME II: THE BIDASSOA TO THE BATTLE OF THE NIVELLE *by F. C. Beatson*—The final phase of the campaign in the Iberian Peninsula.

WELLINGTON AND THE FALL OF FRANCE VOLUME III: THE GAVES AND THE BATTLE OF ORTHEZ *by F. C. Beatson*—The final phase of the campaign in the Iberian Peninsula.

NAPOLEON'S IMPERIAL GUARD: FROM MARENGO TO WATERLOO *by J. T. Headley*—The story of Napoleon's Imperial Guard and the men who commanded them.

BATTLES & SIEGES OF THE PENINSULAR WAR *by W. H. Fitchett*—Corunna, Busaco, Albuera, Ciudad Rodrigo, Badajos, Salamanca, San Sebastian & Others.

SERGEANT GUILLEMARD: THE MAN WHO SHOT NELSON? *by Robert Guillemard*—A Soldier of the Infantry of the French Army of Napoleon on Campaign Throughout Europe.

WITH THE GUARDS ACROSS THE PYRENEES *by Robert Batty*—The Experiences of a British Officer of Wellington's Army During the Battles for the Fall of Napoleonic France, 1813 .

A STAFF OFFICER IN THE PENINSULA *by E. W. Buckham*—An Officer of the British Staff Corps Cavalry During the Peninsula Campaign of the Napoleonic Wars.

THE LEIPZIG CAMPAIGN: 1813—NAPOLEON AND THE "BATTLE OF THE NATIONS" *by F. N. Maude*—Colonel Maude's analysis of Napoleon's campaign of 1813 around Leipzig.

LEONAUR

ALSO FROM LEONAUR

AVAILABLE IN SOFTCOVER OR HARDCOVER WITH DUST JACKET

BUGEAUD: A PACK WITH A BATON *by Thomas Robert Bugeaud*—The Early Campaigns of a Soldier of Napoleon's Army Who Would Become a Marshal of France.

WATERLOO RECOLLECTIONS *by Frederick Llewellyn*—Rare First Hand Accounts, Letters, Reports and Retellings from the Campaign of 1815.

SERGEANT NICOL *by Daniel Nicol*—The Experiences of a Gordon Highlander During the Napoleonic Wars in Egypt, the Peninsula and France.

THE JENA CAMPAIGN: 1806 *by F. N. Maude*—The Twin Battles of Jena & Auerstadt Between Napoleon's French and the Prussian Army.

PRIVATE O'NEIL *by Charles O'Neil*—The recollections of an Irish Rogue of H. M. 28th Regt.—The Slashers—during the Peninsula & Waterloo campaigns of the Napoleonic war.

ROYAL HIGHLANDER *by James Anton*—A soldier of H.M 42nd (Royal) Highlanders during the Peninsular, South of France & Waterloo Campaigns of the Napoleonic Wars.

CAPTAIN BLAZE *by Elzéar Blaze*—Life in Napoleons Army.

LEJEUNE VOLUME 1 *by Louis-François Lejeune*—The Napoleonic Wars through the Experiences of an Officer on Berthier's Staff.

LEJEUNE VOLUME 2 *by Louis-François Lejeune*—The Napoleonic Wars through the Experiences of an Officer on Berthier's Staff.

CAPTAIN COIGNET *by Jean-Roch Coignet*—A Soldier of Napoleon's Imperial Guard from the Italian Campaign to Russia and Waterloo.

FUSILIER COOPER *by John S. Cooper*—Experiences in the 7th (Royal) Fusiliers During the Peninsular Campaign of the Napoleonic Wars and the American Campaign to New Orleans.

FIGHTING NAPOLEON'S EMPIRE *by Joseph Anderson*—The Campaigns of a British Infantryman in Italy, Egypt, the Peninsular & the West Indies During the Napoleonic Wars.

CHASSEUR BARRES *by Jean-Baptiste Barres*—The experiences of a French Infantryman of the Imperial Guard at Austerlitz, Jena, Eylau, Friedland, in the Peninsular, Lutzen, Bautzen, Zinnwald and Hanau during the Napoleonic Wars.

LEONAUR

ALSO FROM LEONAUR

AVAILABLE IN SOFTCOVER OR HARDCOVER WITH DUST JACKET

THE LIFE OF THE REAL BRIGADIER GERARD VOLUME 1—THE YOUNG HUSSAR 1782-1807 *by Jean-Baptiste De Marbot*—A French Cavalryman Of the Napoleonic Wars at Marengo, Austerlitz, Jena, Eylau & Friedland.

THE LIFE OF THE REAL BRIGADIER GERARD VOLUME 2—IMPERIAL AIDE-DE-CAMP 1807-1811 *by Jean-Baptiste De Marbot*—A French Cavalryman of the Napoleonic Wars at Saragossa, Landshut, Eckmuhl, Ratisbon, Aspern-Essling, Wagram, Busaco & Torres Vedras.

THE LIFE OF THE REAL BRIGADIER GERARD VOLUME 3—COLONEL OF CHASSEURS 1811-1815 *by Jean-Baptiste De Marbot*—A French Cavalryman in the retreat from Moscow, Lutzen, Bautzen, Katzbach, Leipzig, Hanau & Waterloo.

THE INDIAN WAR OF 1864 *by Eugene Ware*—The Experiences of a Young Officer of the 7th Iowa Cavalry on the Western Frontier During the Civil War.

THE MARCH OF DESTINY *by Charles E. Young & V. Devinny*—Dangers of the Trail in 1865 by Charles E. Young & The Story of a Pioneer by V. Devinny, two Accounts of Early Emigrants to Colorado.

CROSSING THE PLAINS *by William Audley Maxwell*—A First Hand Narrative of the Early Pioneer Trail to California in 1857.

CHIEF OF SCOUTS *by William F. Drannan*—A Pilot to Emigrant and Government Trains, Across the Plains of the Western Frontier.

THIRTY-ONE YEARS ON THE PLAINS AND IN THE MOUNTAINS *by William F. Drannan*—William Drannan was born to be a pioneer, hunter, trapper and wagon train guide during the momentous days of the Great American West.

THE INDIAN WARS VOLUNTEER *by William Thompson*—Recollections of the Conflict Against the Snakes, Shoshone, Bannocks, Modocs and Other Native Tribes of the American North West.

THE 4TH TENNESSEE CAVALRY *by George B. Guild*—The Services of Smith's Regiment of Confederate Cavalry by One of its Officers.

COLONEL WORTHINGTON'S SHILOH *by T. Worthington*—The Tennessee Campaign, 1862, by an Officer of the Ohio Volunteers.

FOUR YEARS IN THE SADDLE *by W. L. Curry*—The History of the First Regiment Ohio Volunteer Cavalry in the American Civil War.

LEONAUR

ALSO FROM LEONAUR
AVAILABLE IN SOFTCOVER OR HARDCOVER WITH DUST JACKET

IRON TIMES WITH THE GUARDS *by An O. E. (G. P. A. Fildes)*—The Experiences of an Officer of the Coldstream Guards on the Western Front During the First World War.

THE GREAT WAR IN THE MIDDLE EAST: 1 *by W. T. Massey*—The Desert Campaigns & How Jerusalem Was Won---two classic accounts in one volume.

THE GREAT WAR IN THE MIDDLE EAST: 2 *by W. T. Massey*—Allenby's Final Triumph.

SMITH-DORRIEN *by Horace Smith-Dorrien*—Isandlwhana to the Great War.

1914 *by Sir John French*—The Early Campaigns of the Great War by the British Commander.

GRENADIER *by E. R. M. Fryer*—The Recollections of an Officer of the Grenadier Guards throughout the Great War on the Western Front.

BATTLE, CAPTURE & ESCAPE *by George Pearson*—The Experiences of a Canadian Light Infantryman During the Great War.

DIGGERS AT WAR *by R. Hugh Knyvett & G. P. Cuttriss*—"Over There" With the Australians by R. Hugh Knyvett and Over the Top With the Third Australian Division by G. P. Cuttriss. Accounts of Australians During the Great War in the Middle East, at Gallipoli and on the Western Front.

HEAVY FIGHTING BEFORE US *by George Brenton Laurie*—The Letters of an Officer of the Royal Irish Rifles on the Western Front During the Great War.

THE CAMELIERS *by Oliver Hogue*—A Classic Account of the Australians of the Imperial Camel Corps During the First World War in the Middle East.

RED DUST *by Donald Black*—A Classic Account of Australian Light Horsemen in Palestine During the First World War.

THE LEAN, BROWN MEN *by Angus Buchanan*—Experiences in East Africa During the Great War with the 25th Royal Fusiliers—the Legion of Frontiersmen.

THE NIGERIAN REGIMENT IN EAST AFRICA *by W. D. Downes*—On Campaign During the Great War 1916-1918.

THE 'DIE-HARDS' IN SIBERIA *by John Ward*—With the Middlesex Regiment Against the Bolsheviks 1918-19.

LEONAUR

ALSO FROM LEONAUR
AVAILABLE IN SOFTCOVER OR HARDCOVER WITH DUST JACKET

CPSIA information can be obtained at www.ICGtesting.com
Printed in the USA
LVOW091359171111

255442LV00001B/9/P